Twayne's United States Authors Series

Sylvia E. Bowman, *Editor*

INDIANA UNIVERSITY

James Russell Lowell

JAMES RUSSELL LOWELL

by

Claire McGlinchee

An important figure in his own time, ninteenth-century America, James Russell Lowell merits the attention of the twentieth. In this study, Lowell is presented as one of America's few great men of letters, and this assertion is substantiated by a careful consideration of both Lowell's literary work and his career.

His poetry was first known to his classmates at Harvard, and Lowell is, in the popular imagination, best remembered as a poet. He was also a satirist, who used colloquial language with skill to criticize the United States' war with Mexico (Biglow Papers, 1848). The service he did for the American vernacular, says Professor McGlinchee, is a major contribution to the linguistic history of this country.

As a professor at Harvard, the first editor of the *Atlantic Monthly*, and Minister to Spain, Lowell gained much for the cause of American literature and culture, helping to establish European respect for the New World's arts. Claire McGlinchee suggests that his best work was "not of an age but for all time."

JAMES RUSSELL LOWELL

By CLAIRE McGLINCHEE

Hunter College

 120

CARNEGIE LIBRARY
LIVINGSTONE COLLEGE
SALISBURY, N. C. 28144

Twayne Publishers, Inc.   ::   New York

Copyright © 1967 by Twayne Publishers, Inc.

All Rights Reserved

Library of Congress Catalog Card Number: 67-13185

MANUFACTURED IN THE UNITED STATES OF AMERICA BY
UNITED PRINTING SERVICES, INC.
NEW HAVEN, CONNECTICUT

811.3
M 145

74193

74193

To
CONNIE

ABOUT THE AUTHOR

CLAIRE MCGLINCHEE is, as Lowell was, strongly rooted in a New England background. Born in Boston, she spent much of her early life in Boston, Cambridge, and Concord, cities still permeated with a unique atmosphere. She is the author of *The First Decade of the Boston Museum* and her articles have appeared in *Musical Quarterly* and the *Shakespeare Quarterly,* among others. Professor McGlinchee (Ph.D.—Columbia University) has also published a large number of reviews for the *New York Times,* the *New England Quarterly,* and *America.* She pursues her academic career at Hunter College as Professor of English.

Preface

JAMES RUSSELL LOWELL was one of the giants of New England's flowering years. His work represents the versatility implied in the title Man of Letters. As such, he gained a prominence that his contemporaries working in a single form of expression could not achieve. Other aspects of Lowell's life—his lectureships, editorships, distinguished performance in the diplomatic world, which today would be regarded as good public relations—kept his illustrious name constantly before the public yet placed him near the slippery brinks of reputational disaster. He acquitted himself nobly, increasing the high esteem he had won through his fulfillment of each assignment, for he skillfully and tactfully avoided the pitfalls.

So intimately, indeed, so inseparably are Lowell's poetry and prose the reflection of his life that in writing a critical analysis of his work, the warp of biography is inevitably interwoven with the woof of analysis. For that reason, although critical-analytical commentary has been made, one must recognize the fact that there is not enough depth or difficulty to Lowell to warrant extended explication and analysis.

I have presented my material as follows: In Chapter I, I give a brief indication of the state of American literature at Lowell's birth in 1819; and I have emphasized the coincidental birth and death dates of Lowell, Melville, and Whitman, whose lives and genius are almost completely different. I give briefly in Chapters II and III a chronological account of significant events in Lowell's life to the year 1860. Chapter IV is devoted to the early poems, consisting mostly of miscellany and the still popular "Vision of Sir Launfal." I feel that Lowell's self-critical attitude toward this early work is indicative of what I stress in Chapter V, the theme of which is Lowell the Critic, manifested essentially in the "Fable for Critics," letters, Among My Books (2 volumes), and My Study Windows. It seemed to me that a chapter should be devoted to Professor Lowell. Though he himself thought he "was never good for much as a professor," Barrett Wendell found him the "most human instructor" and the "most inspiring teacher." This is the subject of Chapter VI.

Lowell lived through the disturbed years of two wars, the Mexican War of 1848 and the Civil War. In Chapter VII, "Political Writings," I stress his political verse, particularly the two series of *Biglow Papers*. I have mentioned a goodly number of the prose essays on politics, but they have not, in my estimation, had the influence on American and English thinking that the *Biglow Papers* have. The last three chapters are divided as follows: Chapter VIII covers Lowell's career as a diplomat in Spain and England; Chapter IX relates his last years when he returned to a vastly changed America, to fit into a society from which were missing many of his dearest friends; to lecture, read, edit the great volume of work he had accomplished, and to write some late poems. The final chapter evaluates his later poetry, "The Cathedral" and the odes.

Anybody re-reading Lowell's complete works in the 1960's will find many arid pages. He will also be pleased to realize that the finest works pass the "sterling" test; their lustre has not dulled. Best of all, Lowell the *man* steps forth from the pages of his works and from previous studies of him as a princely figure— aristocratic, urbane, dignified; loving and lovable; long-suffering in tragedy; irrepressible as a humorist—the perfect humanist.

Wherever possible in the study, I have let Lowell speak for himself from his letters and lesser known articles. This seemed the best way to enable the reader to feel Lowell as close as I did while I was writing.

In pursuing the research necessary to produce this book, I found a true Lowellian graciousness and helpfulness in librarians at Harvard University, Hunter College, and the Boston Public Library; in Mr. Thomas Delporte, curator of the treasures at Craigie House; in Mrs. Franklin Ford, who took me on a tour of Elmwood while it was being readied for the family of Dean Ford of Harvard; in fellow scholars and friends, especially Arthur Colby Sprague and Thomas Ollive Mabbott; in Harper and Row for permission to quote from the two volumes of letters edited by Charles Eliot Norton and from *Literary Friends and Acquaintance* by Howells; in Houghton Mifflin Company for

Courtesy of New York Public Library

JAMES RUSSELL LOWELL

permission to quote from Scudder's biography, Greenslet's American Men of Letters biography, *The Complete Poetical Works of James Russell Lowell,* Edward Everett Hale's *James Russell Lowell and His Friends* and to use the Rowse crayon of Lowell from the last named volume, and particularly in the helpful editorial comments of Professor Sylvia Bowman and the generous patience, critical eye, and willing ear of my sister.

CLAIRE McGLINCHEE

Hunter College

Contents

Chronology

1819   James Russell Lowell born February 22 in Cambridge, Massachusetts, at Elmwood.

1827- Attended in Cambridge school kept by Mr. William Wells.
1834

1834   Entered Harvard College.

1837   Poems and articles published in *Harvardian*.

1838   Graduated from Harvard College; class poem published.

1839   Studied law at Dane College Law School.

1839- Poems published in the *Southern Literary Messenger*.
1840

1840   Received law degree from Dane College. In August, became engaged to Maria White of Watertown.

1841   First volume of Poems, *A Year's Life*.

1841- Poems and articles appeared in the *Boston Miscellany*,
1842   *Arcturus, Graham's Magazine*, the *National Anti-Slavery Standard*, the *U.S. Magazine and Democratic Review*, and the *Liberty Bell*.

1842   *The Old English Dramatists* in the *Boston Miscellany*. I, II and III.

1843   Published his own journal, *The Pioneer*, with Robert Carter; only three numbers issued. *Poems*, a volume published by John Owen.

1844   Articles and poems in the *Boston Courier*, the *North American Review, Graham's Magazine*, the *Liberty Bell*. Prose volume: *Conversations on Some of the Old Poets*. On December 26, married Maria White.

1845   Lowell and Maria went to Philadelphia to live. Articles and poems in *Graham's*, the *Broadway Journal*, the

Pennsylvania Freeman, the *Boston Courier,* the *American Review,* the *Liberty Bell.* Returned to Elmwood in May; December 31, the first child, a daughter, Blanche, born at Elmwood.

1846 June 17, the first *Biglow Paper* appeared in the *Boston Courier.* Articles and poems in the *Anti-Slavery Standard.*

1847 Death of Blanche in March. Three more *Biglows* in the *Boston Courier;* articles and poems in *North American Review,* the *People's Journal,* the *Liberty Bell,* the *Pennsylvania Freeman.* Birth of Mabel, in September.

1848 *Poems: Second Series.* Reviews in *Massachusetts Quarterly Review,* and the *Standard. Biglows* V–IX in *Standard* and *Courier. The Biglow Papers, First Series* published complete. *The Fable for Critics. The Vision of Sir Launfal* (Dec. 17, 1848).

1849 Corresponding editor of *Anti-Slavery Standard.* Articles and poems largely on Abolition in the *Standard,* a few in the *North American, Massachusetts Quarterly,* and the *Liberty Bell.* Third daughter, Rose, born July 16.

1850 Death of Rose, February. Political articles and poems in *Graham's,* the *Standard,* the *Courier,* and the *Boston Daily Advertiser.* Death of Lowell's mother, March 30. Lowell's only son, Walter, born in December.

1851 A few poems in *Graham's,* the *Standard;* first trip abroad, July to October, 1852. Walter died in April, 1852.

1853- "A Moosehead Journal": *Putnam's Magazine.* Publication
1854 largely in *Putnam's* and *Graham's. Fireside Travels:* in *Putnam's,* April and May. *Leaves from My Italian Journal* in *Graham's* in April, May, July. Death of Maria White Lowell, October 27, 1853; summer spent at Beverly with Mrs. Charles Lowell; series of lectures at the Lowell Institute in Boston.

1855 Poetry in *Graham's* and in the *Crayon,* especially the *Pictures from Appledore.* January, publication of a volume of Maria Lowell's poems.

1855- In Europe, preparing for his Harvard lectureship; August
1856 1856, returned to Cambridge, living in the home of his brother-in-law, Dr. Estes Howe, on Kirkland Street, his home until January, 1861. Succeeded Longfellow as Smith Professor of Modern Languages at Harvard.

1857 Editor of the *Atlantic Monthly;* contributed articles and poems to this publication. Married Frances Dunlap in September.

1858 Frequent articles and poems in the *Atlantic.*

1859 Largely reviews in the *Atlantic.*

1860 Articles and reviews in the *Atlantic.*

1861 January: death of Lowell's father, the Reverend Charles Lowell. In May, Lowell gave up his editorship of the *Atlantic;* continued contributions until 1864. Lowell moved back to Elmwood.

1862- Second Series of *Biglow Papers* appeared in the *Atlantic.*
1863

1864 Began editing the *North American Review* in January. Wrote articles and reviews largely for this publication, but a few still appeared in the *Atlantic. Fireside Travels.*

1865- Reviews, articles, and poems in the *North American,* the
1868 *Atlantic,* and the *Nation* (1865); the *Commemoration Ode.* 1868: *Under the Willows and Other Poems.*

1869- Book reviews, essays, and occasional poems in the *Atlantic*
1870 and in the *North American.*

1870 *The Cathedral:* long poem on visit to Chartres Cathedral. *Among My Books:* series of essays.

1871 *My Study Windows:* series of essays. In April, Mabel Lowell was married to Edward Burnett.

1872 Two essays in *North American.* Third trip to Europe.

1873 Went to England in the spring to receive an honorary degree at Oxford of Doctor of Canon Law.

1874 Three poems in *Atlantic* and *North American*. Received Doctor of Law degree at Cambridge, England, in June.

1875 Poems in the *Atlantic* and the *Nation*.

1876 Reviews and poems in the *Nation* and the *Atlantic*. *Among My Books: Second Series*.

1877 Miscellanies in *Atlantic* and *Nation*. *Three Memorial Poems*. Minister to Madrid (1877-1880).

1880- Minister to the Court of St. James.
1885

1884 Speech on *Democracy* at Birmingham, England, October 6.

1885 Death of Frances Dunlap Lowell, February 19. Lowell returned to America in June.

1885- Professor Emeritus at Harvard; winter at Southborough
1886 with his daughter, Mabel Lowell Burnett.

1886 Spent the summer in England. November: delivered address at 250th anniversary of Harvard. Published *Democracy and Other Addresses*.

1887 Spring series of lectures on the old dramatists at the Lowell Institute in Boston. In England in the summer.

1888 *Political Essays. Heartsease and Rue:* volume of poems. Again went to England for the summer.

1889 Address on "Our Literature" at New York celebration of the centenary of Washington's Inaugural. Last visit to England in May; moved back to Elmwood in the autumn of this year. "The Study of Modern Languages": address before the Modern Language Association of America.

1890 Saw completed ten-volume edition (Riverside) of his complete works.

1891 Death of Lowell on August 12 at Elmwood.

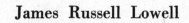

James Russell Lowell

CHAPTER *1*

American Literature at Lowell's Birth

" 'Stand, and deliver a literature!' "[1]

THE YEAR 1819, the birth year of James Russell Lowell, was significant in American literature not only for that fact; it also witnessed the births of Herman Melville and Walt Whitman. But it was not a year in which many important literary works appeared; Bryant's "Thanatopsis" and "Inscription for the Entrance to a Wood," had been published in the *North American Review* in September, 1817, and in the following year "To a Waterfowl" was printed in the same magazine. Willard Phillips, Richard H. Dana, and Edward T. Channing, the three editors, thought the first two poems too good to have been done by an American poet. Irving's *Sketch Book* appeared in installments in America during 1819 and 1820, and as a book in England in 1820. James Fenimore Cooper began to write *Precaution* in 1819 and published it in 1820. Far from a great book, it was important in commencing Cooper's career as a novelist. *The Spy*, which appeared in 1821, had been printed in three editions by the summer of 1822 and was dramatized that same year.

Charles Brockden Brown's career was over with his death in 1810. And the American drama, which had made a feeble beginning before the end of the eighteenth century with Thomas Godfrey's *The Prince of Parthia* and Royall Tyler's *The Contrast* (1787) had advanced little in John Howard Payne's *Brutus or the Fall of Tarquin,* which was performed at Drury Lane in 1818 and continued to be played for sixty years by such actors of the time as Edmund Kean, Edwin Forrest, Junius Brutus Booth the Elder, and Edwin Booth.

Most of the men who were to be Lowell's distinguished contemporaries were too young to have done more than write a first poem or two. Emerson, born in 1803, would graduate from Harvard in 1821, the year he wrote his prize essay on "The Present State of Ethical Philosophy." Hawthorne, born in 1804, would not be graduated from Bowdoin until 1825, nor publish until his romance *Fanshawe* was printed in 1828. His classmate Longfellow had his first poem, "The Battle of Lovell's Pond," published when he was not yet fourteen in the *Portland Gazette* of November 17, 1820. Whittier, born in 1807, the same year as Longfellow, was living in Haverhill and publishing first verses in the *Newbury Free Press*. Oliver Wendell Holmes and Edgar Allan Poe, ten years Lowell's seniors, were not to appear in print until the mid-1820's—Holmes with a brief translation of the *Aeneid* (1825), Poe with his first volume of verse, *Tamerlane and Other Poems* (1827).

It is clear that 1819 was a lean year in American letters. And the three men born in 1819—Lowell on February 22, Whitman on May 31, Melville on August 1—were vastly different in circumstances and in their talents. Melville expressed the history of his time less than the other two did. It was the novelty of the exotic settings in his early novels that made them popular. Not until *Moby Dick* did he memorialize anything so typically American as the whaling industry. But this, his masterpiece, did not receive due recognition until 1919, the centenary of his birth. Walt Whitman sounded in his "barbaric yawp" all of America, covering a span of her territory that only he of the three knew at first hand. He it was, alone of American writers, who answered Emerson's plea of 1837 for the nation to express herself; he it was who reiterated that plea in 1871. But his talent, greater in some ways than Lowell's, was slow in flowering. Whitman published nothing significant until the first printing of *Leaves of Grass* in 1856. Lowell was well known seven years earlier when he had in print two volumes of verse, "The Vision of Sir Launfal," "The Fable for Critics," and the First Series of *Biglow Papers.*

In the "Fable" in 1848 when he was just under thirty years of age and again in "Agassiz" in 1874 when he was fifty-five and wrote briefer but more mellow observations about a selected few, Lowell gave memorable estimates of his contemporaries. Through the years he had virtually nothing to say other than in letters and in prose writings about the subject of American literature until one of his last public addresses, the one given before the Copyright League at Chickering Hall, New York, on November 28, 1887, which was prefaced with a brief but cogent résumé of American literary production. It seems appropriate to quote parts of what he said. After noting that, when he was beginning life, cultivated Americans who heard the question "Who reads an American book?" felt a resentful but helpless anger, he said:

We had no national unity, and therefore no national consciousness, and it is one of the first conditions of a virile and characteristic literature that it should feel solid and familiar earth under its feet. New England had indeed a kind of unity, but it was a provincial unity, and those hardy commonwealths that invented democracy were not and could not yet be quite in sympathy with the new America that was to adopt and expand it. Literature thrives in an air laden with tradition, in a soil ripe with immemorial culture, in the temperature, steady and stimulating, of historic associations. We had none of these. What semblance we had of them was English, and we long continued to bring earth from the mother-country to pot our imported plants with, as the crusaders brought home that of Palestine to be buried in. And all this time our native oak was dropping its unheeded acorns into the crannies of the rock where by and by their sturdy roots would make room for themselves and find fitting nourishment.

Never was young nation on its way to seek its fortune so dumbfounded as Brother Jonathan when John Bull, presenting what seemed to his startled eyes a blunderbuss, cried gruffly from the roadside, "Stand, and deliver a literature!" He was in a "pretty fix," as he himself would have called it. After fumbling in all his pockets, he was obliged to confess that he hadn't one about him at the moment, but vowed that he had left a beautiful one at home which he would have fetched along—only it was so everlasting heavy. If he had but known it, he carried with him the pledge of what he was seeking in that vernacular phrase "fix" which showed that he could invent a new word for a new need without asking leave of anybody.

After enumerating the relatively scant achievements of Irving, Hawthorne, Emerson, Longfellow, Bryant, and Holmes, Lowell continued:

That old question, once so cruelly irritating, because it was so cruelly to the point, has long ago lost its sting. When I look round me on this platform, I see a company of authors whose books are read wherever English is read, and some whose books are read in languages that are other than their own. The American who lounges over an English railway-book-stall while his train is making-up sees almost as many volumes with names of his countrymen on their backs as he sees of native authors. American Literature has asserted and made good its claim to a definite place in the world. Sixty years ago there were only two American authors, Irving and Cooper, who could have lived by their literary incomes, and they fortunately had other sources of revenue. There are now scores who find in letters a handsome estate. Our literature has developed itself out of English literature, as our political forms have developed themselves out of English political forms, but with a difference. Not as parasitic plants fed from the parent stock, but only as new growths from seeds the mother tree has dropped, could they have prospered as they have done. And so our literature is a part of English literature and must always continue to be so, but, as I have said, with a difference. What that difference is, it would be very hard to define, though it be something of which we are very sensible when we read an American book. We are, I think, especially sensible of it in the biography of any of our countrymen, as I could not help feeling as I read that admirable one of Emerson by Mr. Cabot. There was nothing English in the conditions which shaped the earlier part of Emerson's life. Something Scottish there was, it may be said, but the later life at Concord which was so beautiful in its noble simplicity, in its frugality never parsimonious, and practised to secure not wealth but independence, that is—or must we say was?—thoroughly American. Without pretension, without swagger, with the need of proclaiming itself, and with no affectation of that commonness which our late politicians seem to think especially dear to a democracy, it represented whatever was peculiar and whatever was best in the novel inspirations of our soil. These inspirations began to make themselves felt early in our history and I think I find traces of their influence even so long ago as the "Simple Cobbler of

Agawam," published in 1647. Its author, Ward, had taken his second degree at Cambridge and was a man past middle life when he came over to Massachusetts, but I think his book would have been a different book had he written it in England. This Americanism which is there because it is expected of us, gives, I think, a new note to our better literature and is what makes it fresh and welcome to foreign ears. We have developed, if we did not invent, a form of racy, popular humor, as original as it is possible for anything to be, which has found ideal utterance through the genius of "Mark Twain." I confess that I look upon this general sense of the comic among our people and the ready wit which condenses it into epigram, as one of the safeguards of our polity. If it be irreverent it is not superstitious; it has little respect for phrases; and no nonsense can long look it in the eye without flinching."[2]

Almost exactly twenty-five years earlier, Lowell had written to Howells—November 2, 1865—a letter praising the younger man's articles in the *Nation:*

You are doing just what I should wish you to do. The danger of our literature (with plenty of talent) seems to me to be carelessness and want of scholarly refinement. That is the rock I see ahead just now, and I fear we may go to pieces on it if we don't look sharp . . . what I feel is . . . that we especially need refinement in this country as a prophylactic against democracy misunderstood. And as for really good things, that is true here which is true everywhere—they cannot be made by any but those who have served a long apprenticeship—longer, it may be here than elsewhere, since we have less hereditary and accumulated culture. . . ."[3]

At another time Lowell wrote in "The Function of the Poet":

Till America has learned to love art, not as an amusement, not as the mere ornament of her cities, not as a superstition of what is *comme il faut* for a great nation, but for its humanising and ennobling energy, for its power of making men better by arousing in them a perception of their own instincts for what is beautiful, and therefore sacred and religious, and an eternal rebuke of the base and worldly, she will not have succeeded in that high sense which alone makes a nation out of a people, and raises it from a dead name to a living power.[4]

CHAPTER 2

Life of James Russell Lowell–
1819 to 1853

"Sometimes my bush burns, and sometimes it is
A leafless wilding shivering by the wall, . . ."[1]

ELMWOOD, the place of Lowell's birth, was to be that of his death. The poet came of a long line of illustrious forebears, for the names Lowell and Perceval are in the Battle Abbey Roll of the early Normans who came to England with William the Conqueror. His father, the Reverend Charles Lowell, pastor of West Church on Cambridge Street in Boston, was fifth in descent from Percival Lowell, who came to this country in 1639 and who spelled the name "Lowle." The first poet to appear in an illustrious dynasty that was heretofore composed largely of clergymen, lawyers, college presidents, and occasionally of successful businessmen, James Russell Lowell apparently inherited his gift and the romantic side of his nature from his mother, Harriet Traill Spence, who was descended on both sides of her family from Orkney Islanders. This descent gave her a heritage in ballad lore and a penchant for occultism that she passed on to young James. Like Milton, Cowley, and Keats, three of Lowell's many poetic gods, he "first looked into Spenser's *Faerie Queene*" and found there the pictorial as well as the rhythmic beauty that was to lead him to call Spenser "the poet's poet" and that, later, was to mark his own writing.

James's future ability as an orator he owed to his father, who was noted among his congregation for the charm of his utterance from the pulpit. It was through personal charm that the poet, as minister to Spain and to the Court of St. James, gained an enviable popularity and ranked near the top of the list of outstanding American diplomats.

When Lowell was born at Elmwood, the family had been there only a year. This home figures conspicuously in the early poems and essays. Standing today, though no longer in possession of the Lowell family, it is, with its neighbor Craigie House, one of the principal historical houses of old Cambridge.[2] The fine old elm trees and the pines attracted many birds; and as he read in the great library in his boyhood, Lowell felt these creatures of nature very close to him. He was to write of them many times in his poems, in his essays "My Garden Acquaintance" and "Cambridge Thirty Years Ago" which dates 1854, and in his letters.

William Dean Howells, who, in his own words, ". . . did genuinely love the elmy quiet of the dear old Cambridge streets" and who "had a real and instant pleasure in the yellow colonial houses, with their white corners and casements and their green blinds, that lurked behind the shrubbery . . ."[3] was to be a frequent visitor at the Lowell home. Of Elmwood he had this to say:

> All was of a modest dignity within and without the house, which Lowell loved but did not imagine of a manorial presence; and he could not conceal his annoyance with an over-enthusiastic account of his home in which the simple chiselling of some panels was vaunted as rich woodcarving. There was a graceful staircase, and a good wide hall, from which the dining-room and drawing-room opened by opposite doors; behind the last, in the southwest corner of the house, was his study.[4]

Later, two years before Lowell's death, Howells was again at Elmwood:

> At such times I found him sitting in the room which was formerly the drawing-room, but which had been joined with his study by taking away the partitions beside the heavy mass of the old colonial chimney. He told me that when he was a new-born babe, the nurse had carried him round this chimney for luck, and

now in front of the same hearth, the white old man stretched himself in an easy-chair, with his writing-pad on his knees and his books on the table at his elbow, and was willing to be entreated not to rise. I remember the sun used to come in at the eastern windows full pour, and bathe the air in its warmth.[5]

I *Education*

At the private boarding and day school kept near his home by William Wells, an Englishman, Lowell was well trained in the classics. It was there, too, that he met such lifelong friends as William Wetmore Story and Colonel Thomas Wentworth Higginson. At fifteen, Lowell went to Harvard College, then a small institution of two hundred students. George Ticknor, who was teaching modern languages at the time, was to be succeeded when Lowell was in his third year by Longfellow, who in turn would be succeeded by Lowell in 1856. Josiah Quincy, president of Harvard during Lowell's student days, was to be the subject of "A Great Public Character," one of the poet's best essays. These days at Harvard were long before the elective system of studies was introduced. Rigid requirements of Latin, Greek, and mathematics prevailed, and he was to recommend a return to this system later in his life.

Essentially shy and emotional, Lowell was occasionally the extreme extrovert. An omnivorous reader, he especially liked Dante, Tasso, Spenser, Shakespeare, Milton, Butler, the Romantic poets, Carlyle, Landor, Montaigne, and Hakluyt's *Voyages*. Highly sensitized, he reflected the prevailing "sensibility" that was felt in America in the early decades of the nineteenth century and which dominated England during the second half of the eighteenth. There was always in his nature a fortunately generous share of "the saving sense" which kept his character free from the danger of imbalance. This quality he was to need as woes trod upon one another's heels in the 1850's and again in later life. In college, his humor showed in the undergraduate affiliations with the Hasty Pudding Club and with the college magazine "Harvardiana." Even this early, a gift for nonsense-writing manifested itself—the seeds, perhaps, of what was to flower into the style of the "Biglow" series in 1848 and in 1860.

That Lowell was not a "college grind" may be judged from a letter his father wrote him from New York in May, 1837, just before he sailed for Europe with Mrs. Lowell for a three years' stay:

> I shall direct Charles to pay you half a dollar a week. If you are one of the first eight admitted to $\phi\beta\kappa$, $1.00 per week, as soon as you are admitted. If you are not, to pay you 75 cents per week as soon as you are admitted. If I find my finances will allow it, I shall buy you something abroad. If you graduate one of the first five in your class, I shall give you $100 on your graduation. If one of the first ten, $75. If one of the first twelve, $50. If the first or second scholar, $200. If you do not miss any exercises unexcused, you shall have Bryant's "Mythology," or any book of equal value, unless it is one I may specially want.[6]

The bait about the volume of Bryant did not attract Lowell, for he scored an enormous number of absences from both classroom recitations and from chapel exercises. This record, capped by indecorum when he did attend evening chapel on the day of his election as class poet, led to a suspension order issued on June 25, 1838, that virtually exiled him to Concord, where he was to be under the specific tutelage of a Mr. Frost until the Saturday preceding Commencement. He found the tutor, the Reverend Barzillai Frost, and his wife pleasant; and it was while in Concord that he met Emerson. At this point, Lowell was far from being a transcendentalist. He took the typically amateurish attitude of aloofness toward Emerson and Thoreau that was to change later when Lowell was mature enough to appreciate both, although he never did have unqualified admiration for Thoreau.

The time of Lowell's exile extended beyond the Class Day on which his poem was read, but he personally had the poem printed and distributed to his classmates and friends. One happy result of the enforced isolation was the amount of time he had for quiet thought, and the distance that could lend objectivity, both of which made this the young man's best poem to date. Furthermore, being an "occasional poem," it gave him an outside impetus to work. Numbers of his best poems all through his life belonged to this category. His satirical barbs were aimed in varied directions—at Emerson and Transcendentalism; at Carlyle among writers; and at Abolition, Temperance, Women's Rights, and Vegetarianism, all causes toward which he was to turn his energies some years later.

Though real and tragic sorrows were to come to him in the 1840's, the exaggerated melancholy of youth, especially poetic youth, shadowed his first two years after graduation. He suffered the "pangs of dispriz'd love," at one time even holding a revolver to his forehead; fortunately, he lacked the courage to pull the trigger. Perhaps his priceless sense of humor stopped him from acting. His other problem was that of finding a profession. He did not follow in his father's footsteps because, while he had a love of preaching and an innate spirituality, he could not bring himself to accept completely the dogmas of any church. All his life, Lowell, though much more tolerant than many of his social class, found the lack of one compelling belief frustrating. A literary career, especially as a *creator* of literature, was regarded then uncertain.

The law seemed of greater promise, and it was imperative that young Lowell be self-supporting. He began his studies at the Dane College Law School in Cambridge; but it was not to prove a satisfying field to him.

Until 1842, when he finally turned his back on the law, he was in a constant state of indecision, as his letters reveal. These were the years, too, when the democratic and humanitarian side of his nature began to grow. The passages on slavery in his notebook for 1838-9 and various sentiments in letters to friends during these years indicate a feeling for the suffering poor and show that the Abolitionist spirit was well-rooted in him even before the eventful date of December 2, 1839, when he met Maria White.

II *Destiny and Inspiration*

Lowell had gone to visit his classmate William A. White at the latter's home in Watertown.[7] He fell in love with his sister immediately. Maria was attractive, refined, and sweet in appearance, as well as a person of brilliant mind and fine character who had a considerable gift for poetry. Lowell was particularly impressed at this first meeting with her ability to repeat verse. The episode supplied the light that led him from the despair of the previous two years to happiness and achievement. Like Romeo, he had languished protractedly over his Rosaline, only to recognize in the first glance at his Juliet that he had found his destiny. He and Maria became engaged in August 1840 when he received his law degree.

Though Maria's poetry never proved significant, a reader of the little volume of her work that Lowell had printed in 1855, two years after her death, can discern a felicity of rhythm and imagery that must have pleased her fiancé. This gift, as well as her sympathetic and loving nature, made her helpful and encouraging to him. Maria White was a member of a group of young people called "the Band" who interested themselves in the multi-faceted movements and philosophies of the day. Lowell and his beloved were of particular interest to this group who in turn stimulated Lowell's genius.

He was not unmindful of his gift for humor and wrote of it in a letter[8] recording that on a particular evening he had recited close to five hundred extempore macaronic verses. There is in such accounts an element of ineffective exaggeration which persisted as a fault of Lowell's even in much later work. But one can forgive the youthful boasting about his own cleverness. He found in "the Band" an audience for his reading of poetry, one sympathetic to his special taste for Shakespeare, Keats, and Tennyson. "The Band," and particularly Maria White, also gave impetus to already expressed feelings for humanity. Earlier sympathies with the less fortunate classes were extraordinary for a person of his background, and these instinctive reactions were expanded by his association with the Watertown group.

By the fall of 1840, he was an active member of the Chardon Street Anti-Slavery Convention. Letters as well as verse henceforth were to reveal his deep concern over slavery. Lowell had satirized in his Class Poem various "movements" of the time, such as women's suffrage and temperance; now he was addressing in public a meeting of the Cambridgeport Women's Total Abstinence Association. He writes happily of this experience, telling of the ease with which he could address a large audience.[9]

The episode is an important illustration of the dichotomy in Lowell's nature—his conservatism and his very definite democratic leanings.

III *Early Publication*

Early contributions of poems to the *Southern Literary Messenger,* in 1840, when he was attempting to practice law with little success, gave the poet encouragement and kudos, but no financial remuneration. The following year, he sent verses to *Graham's Magazine,* had them accepted, and received a modest honorarium. His first volume of poems, published in 1841, was, like most first volumes, of uneven quality. Few of the poems were ever reprinted, but a handful of those inspired by his beloved Maria match his best poetry in quality. Graham's reviewer perceived in this first book the two qualities that were dominant in the poet at the time; he called the writing "humanitarian and idealistic." Lowell enjoyed a considerable degree of immediate success, impressing such younger "minor" talents as Bayard Taylor and gaining newspaper recognition as far away as New York, though the actual financial income was slight.

Other periodicals that accepted poems were the *United States Magazine and Democratic Review* (May, 1842), *The Dial,* and Nathan Hale's *Boston Miscellany.* In the last he printed prose essays as well as poems. The miscellaneous character of the prose is indicated in the titles: "Getting Up," "The First Client," "Married Men," "Disquisition on Foreheads." The titles also hint at the informality of tone and at the light humor that they contained and suggest the variety of familiar essays that were the vogue in England in the days of Lamb, Hazlitt, and Leigh Hunt. The four essays on Elizabethan dramatists, such as Chapman, Webster, Ford, and Massinger, were appreciative and well-filled with discerningly selected passages quoted from the plays. They show more taste than critical acumen and reveal Lowell's ability even at this early stage to make the dramatists themselves emerge from their writings.

Allegedly, Lowell wrote much of the early work during idle hours in his law office, but he found the surroundings confining and lacking in inspiration. As the year 1842 came to an end, he made the inevitable decision to give up the law. His first new venture was a precarious one, that of founding "the great American magazine," which he named *The Pioneer*. Robert Carter of Cambridge, a journalist of some slight experience, joined forces with him. Leland and Whiting of Boston were its proprietors. Its aims were expressed in the prospectus:

> The object of the subscribers in establishing "The Pioneer" is to furnish the intelligent public with a rational substitute for the enormous quantity of thrice-diluted trash in the shape of namby-pamby love tales and sketches which is monthly poured out to them by many of our popular magazines,—and to offer instead thereof a healthy and manly Periodical Literature whose perusal will not necessarily involve a loss of time and a deterioration of every moral and intellectual faculty.
>
> The critical department of "The Pioneer" will be conducted with great care and impartiality, and while satire and personality will be sedulously avoided, opinions of merit or demerit will be candidly and fearlessly expressed.

Among the popular magazines at which Lowell was hitting were *Gleason's Pictorial Fireside Companion* and *Godey's Lady Book*. He planned, as he wrote to Whittier, to pay well for contributions. Hopefully launched in January, 1843, *The Pioneer* published in the three issues that materialized articles, poems, and stories by Poe (who had a similarly disappointing experience in publishing his own journal), Hawthorne, Elizabeth Barrett, W. W. Story, John Neal, John S. Dwight, Jones Very, and Dr. T. W. Parsons.

One unfortunate blow to the success of the journal was the serious eye trouble that beset Lowell shortly after the appearance of the first issue. This necessitated his going to New York for treatment by a famous oculist, one Dr. Elliott. Young Carter was sorely handicapped without his partner's directive genius. With the March issue eight days late, the two young editors were faced with the demand from the publisher for a pre-arranged forfeit under such circumstances of $500. Unable to meet their obligation, they were offered a waiver if they could cut down the number of copies. Because this impaired their credit with their subscribers, they had to accept failure. Lowell's personal share of debts to printers and contributors was $1,800.

Professionally, this bitterly disappointing experience had widened Lowell's acquaintance with his contemporary men of letters. Even the eye trouble, in taking him to New York, gained him the friendship of men such as Nathaniel Parker Willis and Charles F. Briggs, the latter of whom was to be a close friend for life, as was the painter William Page, whose studio Lowell visited often. Lowell dedicated his 1843 volume of poems to Page, and in 1843 Page painted a portrait of Lowell.

When Lowell returned to Elmwood, he found his mother's mind completely disordered, and his oldest sister, Rebecca, in a state bordering on insanity. Since his father spent four days a week in Boston, it was necessary for the poet to remain constantly in the house. These were depressing as well as confining days, but his beloved Maria White comforted him A brief vacation trip to Bangor, Maine, in the autumn, was his only excursion.

The 1843 *Poems*, first series, was printed by John Owen of Cambridge. These poems show a decided advance over those in *A Year's Life*. The range and tone of the work in this volume forecast the later Lowell. The humanitarianism and the essential humor of the poet are both here. "Rhoecus" and "A Legend of Brittany" sustain the familiar classical and medieval material. Some lyrics are intensely subjective. The stronger, more militant Lowell is manifested in "On Reading Wordsworth's Sonnets in Defense of Capital Punishment" and in "A Glance Behind the Curtain." Most reviewers received the book enthusiastically, and Margaret Fuller's observation that ". . . his thoughts sound no depth, and posterity will not remember him" was an unfortunately erroneous judgment; for Lowell, notwithstanding his faults, was perhaps America's most distinguished Man of Letters. The success of the volume made it possible for the poet to plan his marriage for December 26, 1844.

Conversations on Some of the Old Poets, prepared in 1844, but dated 1845, successful in London as well as in the United States, was to see a second edition at home and was to be reprinted in 1862. His preface "To the Reader" expresses tersely the purpose of criticism: "If some of the topics introduced seem foreign to the subject, I can only say that they are not to my mind, and that an author's object in writing criticisms is not only to bring to light the beauties of the works he is considering, but also to express his own opinions upon those and other matters."[10]

His choice of the conversational form (John and Philip are the parties to the dialogue) gave Lowell the opportunity to indulge a penchant for digression. Many of the opinions expressed in this work he held throughout his life. The main figures discoursed upon are Chaucer, Spenser, Chapman, Ford, Taylor, Donne, Marvell, and Keats.

IV *The First Years of Marriage*

A few days after their marriage, Lowell and his bride went to Philadelphia where he was to work as an editorial writer for the *Pennsylvania Freeman* at the incredibly low salary of ten dollars a month. Both young people supplemented this income with the money they received for poems which their friend Charles F. Briggs published in the *Broadway Journal.* Having work accepted for publication, especially by the more widely circulated magazines, meant much to the young writers. But not all the editors paid their contributors. If they did, the sums were small; and frequently, in order to be published and paid, the writer had to agree not to publish anywhere else. The agreement put an unfair restriction on young talent.

Lowell and Maria returned to Elmwood in May, 1845, and lived in a suite of rooms on the top floor of the house. Their first child, Blanche, was born there on December 31, 1845. In 1846, which proved a lean year, he produced only five poems and five articles. It was a happy year, nevertheless; the modest inheritance Maria received from her father's estate made it possible for them to summer in Stockbridge. And Lowell's supreme joy in his little daughter is evident in many of the letters of this period. He wrote of her to Mr. Davis, when she was four months old: "Miss Blanche Lowell, in the freshness of her morning spirits, is, in my opinion, a sight well worth a journey from Philadelphia to look upon. Why, she laughs all over. You can see it through her clothes. The very tips of her toes twinkle for joy. And then there is not a chanticleer in my numerous flock who can compare with her for crowing. She has another grace which I might in modesty omit, but I love truth! She is exceedingly fond of her father."[11]

From February to May 1846, Lowell wrote four articles on anti-slavery for the *London Daily News,* and in June arrangements were made for articles in both prose and verse for the *National Anti-Slavery Standard.* This affiliation was to continue for four years, with Lowell becoming corresponding editor in 1848.

When little Blanche died in March, 1847, the father's heartbreak was revealed in "She Came and Went," "The Changeling," and "The First Snowfall." Before this year was out, in September, a second child and daughter, Mabel, the only one of four children to grow up, was born to the young couple.

This year, too, was one of promise in Lowell's career but not one of prolific writing. It was a kind of vestibule to the "wonderful year" of 1848. Some poems appeared in the *Standard,* and several reviews in the *North American Review,* which he was later to edit; the first work was done on the "Fable for Critics," and three more "Biglow Papers" were printed in the *Boston Courier.* In the June 17, 1846, issue of the *Courier* appeared the initial letter of Mr. Ezekiel Biglow, Jaalam, to the Honorable Joseph T. Buckingham, editor of the *Courier.* Ezekiel enclosed a poem by his son, Hosea.

V *The Wonderful Year*

No year in Lowell's long and fruitful life was to prove more richly productive than 1848. He was not yet thirty years old and was just ten years out of college. There were some forty articles and poems in magazines and papers and four volumes of poetry, three of them representing his best. Early in this year, *Poems,* second series, appeared; later came the three finest poems—the completed "Fable for Critics"; the *Biglow Papers, First Series;* and "The Vision of Sir Launfal." Practically every quality of the Man of Letters is in these works: the poet, the critic, the letter-writer, the scholar, with much of Lowell's most scintillating wit and his feeling in the reform writing for the less fortunate class. All that he loved at Elmwood, its trees and birds, and its haunting memories, permeate numbers of the more subjective poems in the volume, especially the one called "An Indian Summer Reverie." Lowell the politician and Lowell the author of literary essays were yet to assert themselves impressively. The personal letters of this year are as replete with the work he was doing as he was himself.

The second series of *Poems* was made up largely of verses that he had previously printed in radical papers such as the *Standard*. It is rarely that war poetry or poetry with a social purpose shows much of a divine spark, but Lowell both felt and wrote strongly of the moral and political ills of his day. And occasionally the strong feeling behind his words brought out the strengthening poet within him. "The Present Crisis" shows his power perhaps better than any other poem in the collection.

The poet's pattern of work did not vary greatly throughout his career. He had periods rich in poetic profusion and others when he could find no inspiration or inclination to poetize. The great "Commemoration Ode" presented a block until the night before it was to be delivered, and then words seemed to stream from his pen. In the case of the "Fable for Critics," he wrote several hundred lines virtually at a single sitting, in November, 1847; then, in the following spring, halfway through it, but feeling the poetic impulse wane, he declared to his neighbor Longfellow that he did not intend to write any further poetry— or at least for a number of years, because he could not "write slowly enough." However, Lowell did take up the work at intervals and completed this significant piece of American literary criticism by the end of October of that same year.

The crowning work of Lowell the humorist was to be the *Biglow Papers,* the first set (that dealing with the Mexican War) finished in his *annus mirabilis* and the second series at the time of the Civil War. The entire fabric of this work, in every aspect of characterization and outlook, was as New England Yankee as the dialect he used so skillfully. Dialect as a stylistic device for humor and satiric drive, as well as for local color in both prose and verse, had often marked American writing, some of it post-Lowell—the Uncle Remus tales, the political satires of the beloved Mr. Dooley, the novels of Edward Eggleston, the poems of James Whitcomb Riley, and *Huck Finn* in which one finds Twain's inimitable contrapuntal interweaving of a half dozen or more dialects. Actually, a quick review of distinguished uses of dialect in English literature would result in a very short list. Lowell had been gaining in skill in the use of this style ever since the evening when he had entertained "the Band" in Watertown with his extemporaneous, macaronic effusions. Even today, the mention of Lowell's name to a well-read Englishman will likely as not bring forth an immediate and accurate quotation of some of John P. Robinson's lines.

In 1849, Lowell became corresponding editor of the *Anti-Slavery Standard* at a salary of five hundred dollars a year. He continued to publish both prose and verse in its pages. This year and the one following brought joy and sorrow in quick succession. The third child and third daughter, Rose, was born on July 16, 1849, but she lived only six months. Lowell's mother, who had been institutionalized for a number of years, died a month later. The fourth child and only son, Walter, was born in December, 1850. Finances were low, but somehow Lowell always managed. He himself was in excellent health and was thereby helped to keep up his own spirits.

From the spring of 1849 to that of 1852, he gradually severed his connection with the *Standard*. In May 1849, he was asked to give up half his yearly salary to Edmund Quincy, who henceforth shared with him the position of corresponding editor. Lowell quite understandably objected to this lowered income.

The writing on the *Standard*, even what he referred to as the fagging particulars of editorial writing, had been of value to him in giving certain disciplines that his sometimes too varied prose style needed. He overweighted his articles with a myriad of allusions which troubled the "average" readers. As with Browning, a man of modest background may be flattered when the author assumes his understanding of certain allusions; but, if the frequency of these assumptions begins to embarrass him, he reads elsewhere. Contrariwise, Lowell's more intellectual readers found in *his* editorials what they missed in those of other editors. The highmindedness that kept much that he wrote above ultimate reproach was always present.

Some retrospective self-evaluation belongs to the year 1849. Though only thirty years of age, Lowell prepared a collected edition in two volumes of his poetry, and he omitted much of the dross of earlier publication. He planned a large work that would, if completed, have antedated Longfellow's *Tales of a Wayside Inn.* But though he expressed a determination to finish it at various times, the work—to be called *The Nooning*—was never completed. Narrative verse was not his forte.

In a letter to Briggs, dated January 1850, Lowell outlined the sequence of his poetic themes thus far as Love and Freedom; and he announced his intention of going then "more *wholly* after beauty herself."[12] "The Voyage of Leif," "Pictures from Appledore," and "Fitz Adam's Story," three narratives in the proposed series, appeared in magazines.

VI *The First Trip Abroad*

About this time, Maria Lowell's health began to fail. In the hope that a year or more in Europe would benefit her and fulfill a long-standing wanderlust in her husband, the couple sold some of the acres that belonged to Elmwood and left—with Mabel and Walter, the children's nurse, and a goat—in July 1851. Their first destination was the Mediterranean. They traveled leisurely through Italy, spending most of the winter of 1852 in Rome. The news that Reverend Charles Lowell had suffered a severe paralytic stroke made them consider returning home, but they decided to complete their year abroad. More shattering to them was the sudden loss of the little son Walter in April of that year.

Lowell did almost no writing this year other than letters home and the Italian notebooks. The latter were to rank among the best American travel literature. The strange kinship that he felt with Rome on this first visit is indicated in what he wrote to John Holmes:

> Surely the American (and I feel myself more intensely American every day) is least of all at home among ruins—but he is at home in Rome. I cannot help believing that in some respects we represent more truly the old Roman power and sentiment than any other people. Our art, our literature, are, as theirs, in some sort exotic; but our genius for politics, for law, and, above all, for colonization, our instinct for aggrandizement and for trade, are all Roman. I believe we are laying the basis of a more enduring power and prosperity, and that we shall not pass away till we have stamped ourselves upon the whole western hemisphere so deeply, so nobly, that if, in the far away future, some Gibbon shall muse among our ruins, the history of our Decline and Fall shall be more mournful and more epic than that of the huge empire amid the dust of whose once world-shaking heart these feelings so often come upon me.[13]

The depleted little family regretfully left Rome in the late spring, journeyed northward through the beauties of the Italian Lake Country, Switzerland, Germany, Provence, and France, and reached England late that summer. Lowell loved the English cathedral towns, as well as Cambridge, Oxford, and, of course, London. He was to acquire many cherished friends and later, as Minister to the Court of St. James, to enjoy in England some of his greatest triumphs. Among the early literary friendships were those with John Kenyon and Walter Savage Landor.

When the Lowells left England in October 1852, they had Thackeray and Arthur Hugh Clough as fellow-passengers on the trip home. In spite of this companionship, Lowell felt bored and depressed during the voyage. The foreboding of sorrow that he was experiencing was realized in the dreaded end—Maria Lowell's death—on October 27, 1853. The poet's dreams were haunted at first by his beloved, an experience that eventually brought a kind of solace. Little Mabel, the sole member left to him of the family he had loved so dearly, was the source of his greatest comfort. Eventually, all-healing time helped too; but the pain of this loss was never completely eased.

CHAPTER 3

Life: 1854–1860

"Men follow Duty, never overtake;
Duty nor lifts her veil nor looks behind."[1]

THE PUBLICATION in late 1853 and in early 1854 of the
travel writings, A Moosehead Journal in Putnam's Magazine
for November 1853; Fireside Travels in Putnam's for April and
May 1854; and Leaves from My Italian Journal in Graham's
Magazine for April, May, and July 1854 showed a marked advance in his development as a prose writer of importance. This
improvement was good fortune for Lowell, for poetic impulse
seemed lacking.

His spirit was further refreshed by a summer (1854) spent
with his sister-in-law, Mrs. Charles Lowell, at Beverly. On his
return to Elmwood in the autumn, he prepared the little volume
of his beloved Maria's poems which he had printed privately by
the Riverside Press in January 1855. Another absorbing interest was the preparation of his course of lectures on the English
poets, which he was to deliver at the Lowell Institute in Boston
during the season of 1854-55. This first course was eminently
successful. Charles Sumner, Longfellow, and F. H. Underwood
(later Lowell's associate on the Atlantic Monthly), who found
the talks inspiring and delightful, praised the intrinsic merits of
the lectures; the speaker's well-modulated and agreeable voice;
and the substance, the earnestness, the charm of his poetic
imagery. Lowell was to use much of this material in later essays,
and therefore never published them in their original form; but
abridgements or "reports" of them, which had appeared against
his wishes in the Boston Advertiser, were reprinted as Lectures
on the English Poets in 1897.

During this series of Institute Lectures, Lowell was officially notified of his appointment as Smith Professor of the French and Spanish Languages and Literatures and of *Belles Lettres* at Harvard; he was to succeed Longfellow. With the appointment went the same permission Longfellow had had to spend a year in Europe preparing for the assignment. The stipend was only twelve hundred dollars, but it seemed a substantial addition to his private income of half that amount and to the small and occasional payment for miscellaneous publication. Another result of his lectures was a tour through the West, during the spring of 1855. Lowell expressed in a personal letter his hatred of lecturing, yet he found the fee of six hundred dollars and the enthusiastic press notices gratifying.

I   *A Second Year in Europe*

When he was preparing for his year abroad, his friends, including Longfellow and Holmes, gave him a farewell dinner at the Revere House the night before his departure for New York. Arriving in Paris, he remained several weeks there. It was during this stay that he visited Chartres Cathedral and gained the inspiration for his remarkable poem "The Cathedral," written fourteen years later—a poem everyone is advised to read before visiting Chartres.

The Storys were in London; and while he was there, Lowell also enjoyed again many meetings with Thackeray. He left for Dresden late in the summer and spent the winter perfecting his use of German; he also attended lectures on German literature, esthetics, and even anatomy. Letters during this period, interspersed liberally with German phrases, are sprightly and entertaining.

For a respite from study, he went to Italy during the following spring (1856), where he found numbers of his friends: Page, the painter; John Field; the Nortons, and the Storys. A group, consisting of Norton, John Field, and C. C. Black, made a Sicilian journey on mule-back. They wrote a joint manuscript journal which has not been published. The parts in Lowell's handwriting indicate that he was more impressed by the local characters and customs than by the classical atmosphere.

II *Second Marriage*

Returning to Dresden for a few summer weeks, Lowell then went home to Cambridge, arriving in August. From this time until 1861, home was on Kirkland Street in the house of his brother-in-law, Dr. Estes Howe. Elmwood, during that period, because of the poor health of Lowell's father and of his unfortunate sister Rebecca, was not a desirable environment for his little daughter Mabel. The poet, his beloved child, and Miss Frances Dunlap made up his household. Before Maria's death, she had expressed a wish that the little girl might be placed under the care of her dear friend Elizabeth Dunlap. As fate would have it, Elizabeth died shortly after Maria, and her sister Frances took charge. Frances had the exact qualities of calm spirit, poise, capability, and warm understanding that made her an ideal companion for Mabel during her father's absence abroad—and an equally ideal second wife to Lowell when they were married in September 1857. But nobody could ever completely fill in Lowell's life the void left by Maria's death. Frances lacked Maria's creative gift, though her nature was more practical; her critical judgment was helpful to him in his writing, and her gracious companionship was a soothing influence.

The term of Lowell's professorship at Harvard extended uninterruptedly for sixteen years beginning in September 1856. He was possibly the least academic of professors of his day, and reactions to his teaching varied. His "difference" and his ineffable charm won him many admirers. Barrett Wendell, who was to be America's first exchange professor to the Sorbonne, wrote of Lowell as he knew him in the Dante class in 1876.

Lowell taught two courses, one in Dante and one in German literature; and he gave various lectures to the college at large on English poetry and general letters. Later a course in Spanish literature was substituted for the German one, and still later he taught Old French literature. Over the years, he collected an impressive library of about seven hundred volumes dealing with Old French literature. He willed these to Harvard where they are kept as a special collection. Perhaps the most valuable feature of the collection is the series of notes he wrote on the flyleaves, in French when the text was French, and at times in Latin when the text was Latin.[2]

As avid a book collector as a reader, he often read all the works of an author—Euripedes, Terence, Calderon. George Woodberry, whom Lowell employed as a student assistant, tells in his reminiscences of Lowell that the poet's custom was to take the books he looked at down from the shelves and then have his student assistant replace them. When Lowell told young Woodberry never to write an essay on any author of whom he had not read the complete work, Woodberry said, "But you have written an essay on Voltaire." Lowell pointed to his shelves and to the famous Beuchot edition and said that he had read it all.[3] In a letter to Miss Norton in 1874, he states that he spent an average of ten hours a day in this scholarly reading.[4]

Lowell may have disliked public lecturing, but he loved to talk about books with friends such as Leslie Stephen and W. D. Howells, as they have attested. Howells said that, when Lowell quoted from a book, he would get it and read the passage over. His private library numbered well over five thousand volumes. The joys that he found in the hours spent there are the theme of many of the most interesting as well as the happiest of his letters—those written between the time of his second marriage, 1857, and his departure to Spain as minister in 1877. Yet his passion for reading did not shut him off from other normal activities. Always a good walker, two favorite spots to which he went were Beaver Brook in Waverley and Waverley Oaks. He belonged to a Whist Club, the other three of the foursome being Dr. Estes Howe, his brother-in-law, and friends Carter and John Holmes. He belonged to the "Adirondack Club" and took trips with the group each year, enjoying the woods, swimming, and hunting.

III   Editor of the Atlantic Monthly

In 1857, when the Atlantic Monthly came into being, Lowell was its first editor. It is said that he accepted the assignment on condition that Holmes give his Autocrat of the Breakfast Table for publication in its pages. The magazine was launched at a dinner held at the Parker House and attended by Mr. F. H. Underwood, whose brain child the project was; by Holmes,

Emerson, Cabot, Motley, Longfellow; and, of course, by Lowell. The title of the publication was suggested by Holmes, and the publishers were Messrs. Phillips and Sampson. Underwood served in two important capacities, as business manager and as assistant editor. The first issue was published in November.

It must have been gratifying to Lowell, after the disappointing failure of his own magazine, the *Pioneer,* which he had started with the same high ideals as those that motivated the founders of the *Atlantic,* to find himself again at the helm of such an undertaking. He proved an excellent editor and enjoyed the work. He was, of course, singularly fortunate in the illustrious list of contributors upon whom he could draw, names that made the *Atlantic* a peer of the great English reviews. Entertaining, even gay, and edifying, the magazine maintained a high literary level without ever becoming heavy. During the Civil War, as during more recent wars, the tone grew appropriately more serious; but the *Atlantic* never ceased to hold the interest of its loyal readers who chose it because it was a definitely "literary" magazine.

This editorial post markedly increased Lowell's income. He started at a salary of $2,500 and six dollars a page for any contributions of his own. Then his salary was increased to $3,000. In his day this income, and his professorial salary, gave him a comfortable freedom from financial cares. In sheer volume of work, his post was an exacting one. The magazine received about five hundred manuscripts each month, which meant not only an impressive amount of reading but a taxing amount of correspondence with authors. Gradually he felt the pressure of this work. He was too conscientious an editor to neglect his responsibilities to readers, authors, owners, or himself.

One of the happiest diversions during these years were the monthly dinners of the Saturday Club, started in 1859 in Boston. He celebrated the gatherings in the ode on Agassiz's death. Holmes, too, wrote verses on this happy gathering of important writers besides himself, Lowell, and Agassiz—Longfellow, Emerson, Hawthorne, and the "once only" visitor, Thoreau. Much loved as their "editor," as well as their good friend, Lowell was honored by the club with a special celebration on February 22,

1859, his fortieth birthday. From these friends something can be learned of Lowell the man.

Howells wrote of his first meeting with him in 1860, after he had had a poem accepted for the *Atlantic*. He found Lowell serious and coldly pleasant. He had to warm up to one, said Howells, and then

> he made you free of his whole heart; . . . His whole personality had now an instant charm for me; I could not keep my eyes from those beautiful eyes of his, which had a certain starry serenity, and looked out so purely from under his white forehead, shadowed with auburn hair untouched by age; or from the smile that shaped the auburn beard, and gave the face in its form and color the Christ-look which Page's portrait has flattered in it. His voice had as great a fascination for me as his face. The vibrant tenderness and the crisp clearness of the tones, the perfect modulation, the clear enunciation, the exquisite accent, the elect diction—I did not know enough then to know that these were the gifts, these were the graces, of one from whose tongue our rough English came music such as I should never hear again. In this speech there was nothing of our slipshod American slovenliness, but a truly Italian conscience and an artistic sense of beauty in the instrument.[5]

Twenty-seven years later, when Agnes Repplier was thirty, she met Lowell and wrote of him: "The most impressive figure that dawned upon my Boston horizon was Mr. James Russell Lowell. There was nothing to mar the impression. He looked as he should have looked. He spoke as he should have spoken. Distinction marked him as her own, and he responded without effort to her election. Always the centre of interest and attention, no one lost anything by granting precedence to a man so flawlessly urbane."[6]

He was to play an important part in the Civil War with his pen. He referred to the years immediately preceding those of the war as ones of "cloistered studies." But as always with Lowell, periods away from the expression of certain phases of his genius proved to be periods in which, as it were, he was subconsciously gathering strength and power for some of his most effective expression.

At the death of Phillips, in 1859, the copyrights of Phillips, Sampson, and Company, and of the *Atlantic Monthly* were bought by the publishing house of Ticknor and Fields. Lowell continued briefly as editor of the magazine; but he gave up the post in May 1861, when the owners expressed the feeling that it would be better for Fields to assume the editorship in person because he had had such intimate relations with most of the best writers of the day. Since Lowell had begun to feel the pressure of the editorial work, this change was in the nature of a release to him; but, as he wrote to Fields, in a letter: "I doubt if we see the finger of Providence so readily in the stoppage of salary as in its beginning or increment. . . ."[7]

He missed the comfortable affluence of his years in the editorial chair. The cessation of his work as editor did not mean the discontinuance of his own publication in the pages of the *Atlantic*, for he contributed to it until he and Charles Eliot Norton took over the editorship of the *North American Review* in January 1864. This magazine was the chief medium for Lowell's articles and poems. The *North American* was noted for its solemn and severe tone. When Lowell and Norton joined forces, they gave to it something of the gracious readability of the *Atlantic* without even slightly lowering its tone.

IV *Political Articles*

Many of Lowell's articles in the two journals were political. Among the best were four that appeared in the *Atlantic* in 1858 in the April, July, August, and November issues: "Mr. Buchanan's Administration," "The American Tract Society," "The Pocket Celebration of the Fourth," and "A Sample of Consistency." After turning almost exclusively to more literary topics during 1859 and the first half of 1860, he reverted again to politics in "The New Tariff Bill" in the July *Atlantic*, and followed that with "The Election in November" in the October issue. "A Plea for Freedom from Speech and Figures of Speech-Makers," in the December issue, made unfortunate and thinly veiled fun of Wendell Phillips under the name of Philip Vandel.

After the war was actually started, more of Lowell's political articles appeared: "Atlantic," "The Question of the Hours," "*E Pluribus Unum*," "The Pickens-and Stealin's Rebellion," and "Self-Possession vs. Prepossession." "The Washers of the Shroud," one of his greatest war poems, inspiriting and full of noble sentiments, appeared in November 1861.

During the remaining two years on the *Atlantic*, Lowell's war writing was for the most part the second series of *Biglow Papers*, "Two Scenes from the life of Blondel," and a memorial tribute to Shaw. After the shift to the *North American Review*, he wrote largely prose articles: "The President's Policy," "McClellan's Report," "The Rebellion; Its Causes and Consequences," and "The Next General Election" in 1864; "Reconstruction" and "Scotch the Snake or Kill It" in 1865; and "The President on the Stump" and "The Seward-Johnson Reaction" in 1866.

Few American writers have shown the deep concern and acute judgment in respect to political problems that Lowell did. Even the occasional sudden intrusions of the inevitable Lowell humor tended rather to soften hard lines and to salve the hurt than to destroy the dignity of tone that was necessary in these matters. The warmth of his appreciation of greatness when it appeared even from humble background is clearly evident in his early recognition of the greatness of Lincoln, whose candidacy was regarded with the reverse of enthusiasm by the bluebloods of Boston and Cambridge.

When peace was declared in April of 1865, Lowell expressed his reaction in the following words, part of a letter on April 13 to Charles E. Norton: "The news, my dear Charles, is from Heaven. I felt a strange and tender exaltation. I wanted to laugh and I wanted to cry, and ended by holding my peace and feeling devoutly thankful. There is something magnificent in having a country to love. It is almost like what one feels for a woman. Not so tender, perhaps, but to the full as self-forgetful."[8]

Harvard College lost ninety-three sons in the Civil War. She set July 21, 1865, as a day to memorialize these men. Lowell was asked to write the commemorative ode. His concern for the problems of this war, expressed so often and so nobly in many published works in both prose and verse, his personal losses, his patriotism—all equipped him to perform this difficult task. After weeks of inability to write, with the occasion only two days ahead, the floodgates opened, and the noble lines and stanzas fairly poured forth onto the pages in uninterrupted hours of writing. The beautiful strophe on Lincoln was added later. Other than this addition, the Ode stands today in its first form, as happened with much of Lowell's work. Even when he did revise with great care, he often went back to the original form of the work.

Lowell was deeply moved as he spoke his lines, and many in the audience were also. Afterward, he thought the poem had not been an unqualified success. To those who read it today, it is understandable that, even with all that the occasion lent to it, many would find it long and involved. Its finest qualities were better appreciated when it appeared in print with the addition of the truly great lines honoring Lincoln.

Lowell's new editorial duties at the helm of the *North American Review* gave him the opportunity to write some longer papers. As a quarterly, the magazine had space for contributions of fifteen thousand words. By 1876, twelve years after becoming its editor, most of Lowell's best literary essays had been printed in the *Review*, in the *Atlantic* (the shorter ones), and in the *Nation*. "Carlyle's *Frederick the Great*" and "Swinburne's Tragedies" were printed in the *Review* for 1866; "Rousseau and the Sentimentalists" and "Lessing" in 1867. The shorter "A Great Public Character," on President Quincy of Harvard, was sent to the *Atlantic* of November 1864. "Witchcraft," "Shakespeare Once More," and "Dryden" appeared in 1868 in the *Review;* and in the same year in the *Nation* was a brief article, "Mr. Emerson's New Course of Lectures," a piece which Lowell expanded later into one of his most outstanding essays. The charming "A Good Word for Winter" was published in the *Atlantic Almanac* for 1870; "On a Certain Condescension in Foreigners" in the *Atlantic Monthly* during 1869; and the overly harsh review of Hazlitt's "Library of Old Authors" and his own "Chaucer" were in the *Review* of April and July, respectively, 1870. The essay on Pope appeared in the January 1871 issue of the *Review*. His first volume of essays, entitled *Among My Books,* came out in the spring of that year, and a second volume of essays, *My Study Windows* in the autumn. His review of Masson's *Life of John Milton* and of Miss Rossetti's *Shadow of Dante* appeared in 1872.

Two years of European travel interrupted this considerable stream of publication until the printing of the Spenser essay in the April 1875 issue of the *North American*. A third volume of essays, the second series of *Among My Books*, dates from 1876. This marked the completion of his important critical writing except for the latest essays which were published at the end of his life and collected posthumously. There were to be several other volumes of poetry and longer single poems: *Under the Willows and Other Poems* in 1869; "The Cathedral" in 1870; "Agassiz" in 1874; three odes—the "Ode Read at the Concord Centennial," "Under the Old Elm" in 1875, and "Ode for the Fourth of July" in 1876—were published together in his "Three Memorial Poems" in 1877; and the volume *Heartsease and Rue* in 1888.

Somewhat less taxed by such things as the pressures of editorial duties and of an active, full-time professorship, Lowell was freer to enjoy his friends, as his letters to T. B. Aldrich, Thomas Hughes, Leslie Stephen, and C. E. Norton indicate. Hughes had sponsored the *Biglow Papers* in England. On his visits to America, he spent some time at Elmwood, as did Leslie Stephen. Lowell loved his friends and craved affection. In a much-quoted letter to Norton, he wrote: "It is always my happiest thought that with all my drawbacks of temperament (of which no one is more keenly conscious than myself) I have never lost a friend. For I would rather be loved than anything else in the world. I always thirst after affection, and depend more on the expression of it than is altogether wise."[9]

V *Two Years in Europe*

Lowell asked the authorities at Harvard to grant him a tutor to ease his professorial duties. This relief meant, of course, giving up a generous portion of his salary. He thought it wise to establish a permanent income of $5,000 a year by selling some of the acres of the estate at Elmwood in 1871. Even when this income shrank to $4,000, he was still secure from financial worry. Failing to receive two years' absence from Harvard on half-pay, he resigned in the spring of 1872 and sailed on July 9 with Mrs. Lowell on a third trip to Europe. His daughter Mabel was married in April to Edward Burnett of Southborough. He was happy to be present at the wedding and took further joy in the appearance of his "Dante" essay in the *North American* for July.

This two-year visit to Europe was, like the others, a period of virtually no writing other than letters home. Lowell's health, which had been so robust, began to decline. He suffered a good deal from the gout, but discomfort was counteracted by the joy he took in friends, not only the English ones but the American ones who, like himself, were abroad—the Nortons, John Holmes, and the Emersons. On this trip, too, he received two honorary degrees in England, a Doctor of Canon Law from Oxford in 1873 and, just before he sailed home on June 23, 1874, a Doctor of Laws from Cambridge. The summer of 1873 he and his wife were in Switzerland and Germany; from there they went to Venice and then to Florence, where Lowell received the sad news of the death of Louis Agassiz. Much in his stay at the Casa Guidi caused him to live over the earlier visit there with his beloved Maria when Mabel was a tiny child. This emotional surge, and the news of a cherished friend's death, inspired him to write the "Ode to Agassiz," one of his most outstanding poems.

After a month during February and March of 1874 spent in Rome with the Storys, the Lowells returned to their quaint Hotel de Lorraine (at No. 7 rue de Beaune in Paris), always his headquarters in that city.

In spite of the happiness, the enriching experiences, and the honors received on this trip, Lowell was glad to return home and to resume work at Harvard. He also found himself engaged in politics again. He agreed to play an active part in the election of 1876 and spoke eloquently in the quest of "an honest independence in politics, and in particular for civil service reform."[10] He was chosen as a delegate to the Republican Convention in Cincinnati. Hayes defeated Blaine for the nomination on the seventh ballot. Lowell was named one of the presidential electors. He demonstrated his forthrightness and his high principles when he refused to cast his ballot for Tilden to break the deadlock that followed the election, and Hayes's election stood.

CARNEGIE LIBRARY
LIVINGSTONE COLLEGE
SALISBURY, N. C. 28144

CHAPTER 4

Early Poems: Miscellany; 'Sir Launfal'

"Heaven's cup held down to me I drain, . . ."[1]

LOWELL wished to be a poet more than anything else; and, if poetry was not to be his complete destiny, it must be granted that his gift was a considerable one and that at his best American poetry can boast of no better. He was to publish four sizable volumes of verse besides the two long series of *Biglow Papers*, "The Vision of Sir Launfal," "The Cathedral," and "The Fable for Critics." At his death, there were a sufficient number of Last Poems, several of which had been printed during the years after he returned from England, so that Charles Eliot Norton could issue the group in a small volume in 1895.

That Lowell loved poetry more than prose is clear from a letter to Sydney H. Gay, who was a fellow-worker on the *Standard*. He wrote in part: ". . . if I have any vocation, it is the making of verse. When I take my pen for that, the world opens itself ungrudgingly before me, everything seems clear and easy, as it seems sinking to the bottom would be as one leans over the edge of his boat in one of those dear coves at Fresh Pond. But, when I do prose, it is *invita Minerva*. I feel as if I were wasting time and keeping back my message. My true place is to serve the cause as a poet. Then my heart leaps on before me into the conflict."[2] This observation was made in reference to the writing he was about to do for Abolition.

I A Year's Life

Lowell's first printed collection, *A Year's Life*, consisted of poems that had appeared in *The Knickerbocker Magazine*, the *Southern Literary Messenger*, and Boston newspapers. Very few "early works" stand the test of time *in toto*. That Lowell was very conscious of the patent immaturity of much of this work is made evident by the fact that, when he made his first general collection in 1849, he kept only seven of the poems printed in *A Year's Life*. The beauty of one of the enduring ones, "Irene," he attributed to Maria, who is referred to both directly and indirectly in many of these early effusions.

Familiarity with the life of Lowell shows plainly his very deeply affectionate nature. He was truly a family man. It may seem odd to the reader of the early poems that the outpourings of his ardent nature in the early lyrics so rarely strike a responding chord in the heart of his public. His muse was as yet immature in this genre. A few years later, when he published the *Miscellaneous Poems* (1843), there was, for a youth of twenty-four, a striking maturity, a strength of purpose, a bold radicalism that sent sparks from the page. In "A Glance Behind the Curtain," he articulated the ideas on Cromwell that had been in his mind crying for expression on the subject of "Those old Roundheads [that] have never had justice done them."[3] "The Present Crisis," is a poem in which the opening lines express the poet's strength of thought and purpose. This poem was dated December 1844:

> When a deed is done for Freedom, through the broad earth's
> aching breast
> Runs a thrill of joy prophetic, trembling on from east to west,
> And the slave, where'er he cowers, feels the soul within him
> climb
> To the awful verge of manhood, as the energy sublime
> Of a century bursts full-blossomed on the thorny stem of Time.[4]

The volume of his message grows and the feeling deepens as the poet finds the image of Christ close to that of the downtrodden slave:

> By the light of burning heretics Christ's bleeding feet I track,
> Toiling up new Calvaries ever with the cross that turns not back,
> And these mounts of anguish number how each generation
> learned

> One new word of that grand *Credo* which in Prophet-hearts hath
>   burned
> Since the first man stood God-conquered with his face to heaven
>   upturned.[5]

The crescendo continues as the pertinence of applying old modes to new conditions is challenged in the final stanza:

> New occasions teach new duties; Time makes ancient good
>   uncouth;
> They must upward still, and onward, who would keep abreast
>   of Truth;
> Lo, before us gleam her camp-fires! we ourselves must Pilgrims
>   be,
> Launch our Mayflower, and steer boldly through the desperate
>   winter sea,
> Nor attempt the Future's portal with the Past's blood-rusted key.[6]

Lowell never realized to the full his poetic ideals. Since he regarded his own poetry critically, he rarely felt that he had achieved even near-perfection. Yet, paradoxically, when he did rework a poem, he invariably considered his first version as the preferred one, and so it would be printed. The winning charm of "the man himself," the sincerity and earnestness that he never lost, and his deep moral convictions endeared him to his readers. These qualities in his writing even raised the tone of the periodicals in which many of the individual poems and essays first appeared. It has been observed that, though the collected works fill ten volumes, Lowell never wrote a book. In his own words, ". . . it is the poem that keeps the language alive, and not the language that buoys up the poem."[7] Further observations from the same source, the "Essay on Spenser," state:

> If poems die, it is because there was never true life in them, that is, that true poetic vitality which no depth of thought, no airiness of fancy, no sincerity of feeling, can singly communicate, but which leaps throbbing at touch of that shaping faculty, the imagination.[8]

. . . all great poetry must smack of the soil, for it must be rooted in it, must suck life and substance from it, but it must do so with the aspiring instinct of the pine that climbs forever toward diviner air, and not in the groveling fashion of the potato.[9]

Erudition in the poetry, prose, and drama of the world is everywhere manifest. Ferris Greenslet commented aptly that "His five essays, on Chaucer, Spenser, Shakespeare, Dryden, and Pope, are virtually an adequate account of the development of English poetry from Chaucer to Burns."[10] As a result of his knowledge and interest in such literature, much of his poetry was derivative in nature. A degree of eclecticism is a natural feature of formative creative work in any medium. A "bookish lad," who grew up in the library at Elmwood and was read to sleep by an aunt whose lullabies were the timeless rhythms of Shakespeare and Spenser, had received indelible impressions from these and other favorite poets: Keats, Tennyson, Byron, and later Dante. As with others who possess a divine spark of their own, the influence paled as time proceeded; the individuality within then grew stronger and emerged fully established. In steeping himself in the poets and essayists of England and Europe, Lowell was following the trend of his time.

His versatility of taste in reading was equalled by his familiarity with the main poetic forms of the day. He could handle with almost equal success the sonnet, the ode, the elegy, and the idyll. He was less successful in longer poems of a narrative type because he lacked a perceptible dramatic faculty. Even as he wrote and lectured later on the older dramatists, he emphasized passages of sheer poetic beauty rather than giving special notice to the plays as such or to climactic cruxes.

In the poems, as in the letters, there is a feeling of self-consciousness, a lack of the simple, genuine outpouring of sentiment and gentle philosophy that seemed to come from Longfellow's pen. But Lowell's sophisticated, infinitely clever, acutely civilized manner of expression enchanted a large public. Sometimes the erudition clouded, or even completely blocked, sheer esthetic pleasure for the reader. He was word-conscious. He possessed a virtual instinct for philology—as the introductions to some of the *Biglow Papers* attest—and had a mind so stocked with classical and other literary allusions that he sometimes began a poem with a digression. Often interesting in itself, it caused the reader to wonder when, if at all, he would arrive at the subject indicated by the title. Happily Lowell did reach his subject and do it justice, though digressions were frequent. This characteristic was also true of the prose essays and, it is said, of his class lectures at Harvard.

The 1843 volume, called simply *Miscellaneous Poems*, was dedicated to his friend William Page, the artist. The dedicatory letter, dated December 14, 1843, is typical of the deep affection felt for this young man, whom Lowell had met at the home of Maria White. Part of what Lowell wrote might be quoted as illustrative of his evaluation of various estimates of achievement. He did not change the essentials of this judgment as the years passed:

> . . . the humblest man's true admiration is no uncertain oracle of the verdict of Posterity,—the unerring tribunal where Genius is at last allowed the right of trial by its peers, and to which none but sincere and real Greatness can appeal with an unwavering heart. . . . The sympathy of sister pursuits, of an agreeing artistic faith, and, yet more, of a common hope for the final destiny of man, has not been wanting to us, and now you will forgive the pride I feel in having this advantage over you, namely, of telling that admiration in public which I have never stinted to utter in private.[11]

On June 15, 1843, Lowell wrote to G. B. Loring, concerning "A Legend of Brittany," which opened the 1843 volume: "My wings were never so light and strong as now." These words bespeak a joyous spirit; yet, later, in a Prefatory Note, he refers to this legend and most of the other poems in the volume as works which he "would gladly suppress" or put in small print in the appendix. Lowell thought highly of his "Prometheus," which was radical and anti-slavery in its tone. It was done in blank verse; the Brittany legend, in *ottava rima*. Every anthology of American literature includes the gracefully told "Rhoecus," a "fairy legend of old Greece." It is one of Lowell's best poems.

II *"Vision of Sir Launfal"*

The "Vision of Sir Launfal" was apparently one of the first works of his "wonderful year" of 1848, a period that was richer in poetical productivity than any other. The major works written then—"The Vision," the First Series of *Biglow Papers,* and the "Fable for Critics"—established Lowell as America's chief poet. He mentioned "The Vision" as early as the first of February in a letter to C. F. Briggs, in which he said it would probably be published by itself during the summer. "The Vision" actually appeared in mid-December.

The author's note prefixed to the poem indicates briefly the well-known mythology of the San Grael. He mentions the story of Galahad in Book XVII of the romance of King Arthur, and Tennyson's exquisite poem on the theme. Then Lowell adds: "The plot . . . of the following poem is my own, and, to serve its purposes, I have enlarged the circle of the competition in search of the miraculous cup in such a manner as to include, not only other persons than the heroes of the Round Table, but also a period of time subsequent to the supposed date of King Arthur's reign."[12]

The story of the poem is told in two parts, and each has its prelude. The actual narrative is thin, but it is movingly told; and the poem is well structured through parallelism and antitheses which give effective balance. The prelude to Part First is, in fact, a bit longer than the narrative of the legend. Every American school child has memorized the section of the first prelude that contains the lines:

> 'Tis heaven alone that is given away,
> 'Tis only God may be had for the asking.

> And what is so rare as a day in June?
> Then, if ever, come perfect days:[13] . . .

In the antithetical winter of Part Second are the equally famous lines:

> Not what we give, but what we share,
> For the gift without the giver is bare;
> Who gives himself with his alms feeds three,
> Himself, his hungering neighbor, and me [*sic*].[14]

A reader contemplating not this poem alone, but the full scope of Lowell's work in the glorious year of creation, might well find the subterranean passage that Scudder perceived as connecting the *Biglow Papers* with the *Vision:* a moralistic theme of democracy breaks down class distinctions through the old image expressed in the words of Christ—When you do it unto the least of these My brethren, you do it unto Me. The lesson of this poem is certainly "not of an age."

If the critic finds the poem less than perfect, the flaws are those of an overabundant youthful enthusiasm which, if tempered, would rob the work of its essential charm. The mysticism that creates in even the present-day reader a sense of awe was characteristic of the poet, particularly of the young Lowell. William Dean Howells "knew that Sir Launfal must be Lowell in some sort; . . ."[15] Oliver Wendell Holmes, in a letter thanking Lowell for his copy of the "Vision," wrote an interesting critical comment on it in which he pointed out flaws as well as virtues. He took his friend to task for referring to the dandelion in a poem about the far past; he thought the Baltimore oriole out of place in a tableau of a feudal castle. He also indicated some rough spots in the verse. For Holmes the virtues of the "Vision" were:

> Not the picture of June—it has great beauties but some of the discords I have spoken of—not the departing knight (paragraph III, p. 11)—it is bold, spirited, eminently picturesque, but exaggerated; not the leper's speech (p. 13) which reminds me too much of some of our "transcendental" friends.
>
> The *brook* is the most ingenious and exquisitely finished piece of pen fancy work I have seen for a long time.
>
> "Builds out its *piers* of ruddy light" struck me as a fine expression. But paragraph III of part second is eminently beautiful, —the thought is natural and striking, the painting vivid, and the personification of the little spring altogether charming. Paragraph VI of the same part is very striking, and the moral finely enucleated. . . .[16]

The immortal beauty of the June passage is not completely summed up in the unforgettable first line but in the sheer lyric spontaneity that poured forth as the song from a June bird's throat. Lines such as these a poet "must" write. Their mood is as rare as the June day, and such bits are not often repeated in the same man's work. The lines on the brook, the antithesis of the "June" stanza, are, in Holmes's words, a "most ingenious and exquisitely finished piece of pen fancy work. . . ." But Holmes's adjectives express eloquently the lack of the compelling emotion that fairly spilled the "June" stanza on the page.

Lowell himself was pleased with the brook lines and wrote to Briggs of his inspiration for them: "I walked to Watertown over the snow with the new moon before me and a sky exactly like that in Page's evening landscape. Orion was rising behind me, and as I stood on the hill just before you enter the village, the stillness of the fields around me was delicious, broken only by the tinkle of a little brook which runs too swiftly for Frost to catch it. My picture of the brook in 'Sir Launfal' was drawn from it."[17]

Despite Lowell's reception of Holmes's critical comments, Leon Howard found the poet erratic in attitude toward his literary friends and acquaintances, and sensitive to criticism of his own work: "He regularly encouraged editors to criticize or reject his contributions and was regularly offended when they took even the most hesitant and apologetic advantage of the privilege."[18]

Howard's statement, however, seems to contradict what Lowell himself wrote to James B. Thayer on December 8, 1868: "I have never meddled with any criticism of what I write, nor am I very sensitive about it, having long ago made up my mind that whatever was good would make its own way at last."[19]

Even after the successes of his "wonderful year," Lowell was not carried away by any false sense of his importance. In 1850, he wrote to his friend C. F. Briggs: "What I have written will need to be carried down to posterity on the shoulders of better poems written hereafter, and strong enough to carry the ore in the stone which imbeds it. My dear friend—and you are very dear—I am not a fool, at any rate, and I know my own wants and faults a great deal better than any of my critics."[20]

CHAPTER 5

The Critic

"Of keenest wit, of judgment crystal-clear, . . ."[1]

IN A PREFATORY NOTE to a later issue of the "Fable for Critics," Lowell referred to the work as a *jeu d'esprit* that was extemporized, written rapidly for his own amusement without intention to publish. He sent daily installments to his New York friend, Charles F. Briggs, who urged him to print it. Finally the author consented to anonymous publication, and he did not acknowledge the authorship until several others had claimed it. In a letter to Briggs on November 13, 1847, he characterized it as "a rambling, disjointed affair"; but he expressed a conviction that it would "take," if he could get it read. On December 31, he made a present of it to Briggs in a letter:

> I wish you to understand that I make you a New Year's gift, not of the ms., but of the thing itself. I wish you to get it printed (if you think the sale will warrant it) for your own benefit. At the same time I am desirous of retaining my copyright, in order that, if circumstances render it desirable, I may still possess control over it. Therefore, if you think it would repay publishing (I have no doubt of it, or I should not offer it to you) I wish you would enter the copyright in your own name and then make a transfer to me in "consideration of," etc.[2]

The work proved to be one of the poet's best. His innate critical acumen, his sincere intention all through his life to judge the work of others dispassionately, and his almost unique ability to make lasting judgments of contemporaries account for its success. Only occasionally does personal feeling of antipathy color his work. In a letter to Briggs, dated from Elmwood, March 26, 1848, he wrote:

> I think I shall say nothing about Margaret Fuller (though she offer so fair a target), because she has done me an ill-natured turn. I shall revenge myself upon her by writing better. She is a very foolish, conceited woman, who has got together a great deal of information, but not enough *knowledge* to save her from being ill-tempered. However, the temptation may be too strong for me. It certainly would have been if she had never said anything about me. Even Maria thinks I ought to give her a line or two.[3]

In a subsequent letter to Briggs (May 12), Lowell decided to include Miss Fuller:

> I have done, since I sent the first half, Willis, Longfellow, Bryant, Miss Fuller, and Mrs. Child. In Longfellow's case, I have attempted no characterization. The same (in a degree) of S. M. F. With her I have been perfectly good-humored, but I have a fancy that what I say will stick uncomfortably. So will L. M. C. After S. M. F. I make a short digression on bores in general, which has some drollery in it. Willis I think good. Bryant is funny, and as fair as I could make it, immitigably just. Indeed I have endeavored to be so in all. I am glad I did Bryant before I got your letter. The only verses I shall add regarding him are some complimentary ones, which I left for a happier mood after I had written the comic part.[4]

Bryant had thought that Lowell "stole" from him in his "To the Past." Bryant had also written a poem by that title. Lowell, at least momentarily incensed, said further on in the same letter: "When I steal I shall go to a specie-vault, not to a till." Again, he thinks of writing better as the most effective form of revenge: "My next volume will be enough revenge, for it will be better than my last." And to W. J. Stillman he wrote from Elmwood on January 11, 1855: "I am quite sensible now that I did not do Mr. Bryant justice in the 'Fable.' But there was no personal feeling in what I said—though I have regretted what I *did* say because it might seem personal. I am now asked to write a review of his poems for the *North American*. If I do, I shall try to do him justice."[5]

Charles Eliot Norton quotes from a long letter that Leslie Stephen wrote at Norton's request following Lowell's death. In the letter, dated London, February 11, 1892, Stephen mentioned Lowell's "unvarying sweetness and simplicity," his "unmixed kindliness and thorough wholesomeness of nature." "Lowell was so quick at knowing what were the dangerous topics, that I do not think he could ever have given pain unless he felt it to be a duty. Probably an offence to his patriotic sensibilities would have led to a retort, and he had powers of sarcasm which one could not have roused with impunity."[6]

In a series of biographical and critical sketches of "Our Contributors" in the *Southern Literary Messenger*, Lowell wrote of Poe in the issue of February 1845: "Mr. Poe is at once the most discriminating, philosophical, and fearless critic upon imaginative works who has written in America. It may be that we should qualify our remarks a little, and say that he *might be*, rather than that he always *is*, for he seems sometimes to mistake his phial of prussic acid for his inkstand. . . . Mr. Poe has that indescribable something which we have agreed to call genius."[7] This was surely unbiased opinion, for Lowell did not know Poe personally. As he came to know more of him, he disliked what he called grossness and vulgarity in Poe's treatment of Longfellow, and particularly an allusion to Mrs. Longfellow and her children. Briggs tried to explain to Lowell that Poe was alluding to an abstract Mrs. Longfellow since he did not know at the time that Longfellow was married. Lowell held to his objections, however.

There was also a charge of plagiarism uttered against Lowell by Poe which was quite understandably resented. Lowell wrote to Briggs on August 21, 1845:

Poe, I am afraid, is wholly lacking in that element of manhood which, for want of a better name, we call *character*. It is something quite distinct from genius—though all great geniuses are endowed with it. Hence we always think of Dante Alighieri, of Michael Angelo, of Will Shakespeare, of John Milton—while of such men as Gibbon and Hume we merely recall the works, and think of them as the author of this and that. As I prognosticated, I have made Poe my enemy by doing him a service. In the last *Broadway Journal* he has accused me of plagiarism, and *misquoted* Wordsworth to sustain the charge.[8]

At another time he wrote in a letter to I. Henry Hazer, dated Southborough, November 10, 1885: "I have a high opinion of Poe's genius—a very low one of his character. . . ."[9] He estimated Poe in the "Fable" as "Three fifths of him genius and two fifths sheer fudge" and as one "Who has written some things quite the best of their kind,/But the heart somehow seems all squeezed out by the mind."[10] This is about as neat a brief summing up of Poe as one could wish for. Lowell's little sermon to Poe on his hostility toward Longfellow contains an excellent aphorism: ". . . remember that elegance also is force. . . ." Lowell, born to the finest sense of elegance and taste, could never abide the lack of it.

One of the best passages in the "Fable" is the balanced evaluation of Emerson and Carlyle, a long section of point by point contrast. Holmes admired this passage especially. He wrote to Lowell on November 10, 1848:

> I did of course what everybody else does—looked to see if my own name was in the volume for good or evil,—but in doing so I saw enough to make me begin and go straight through it,—a thing I am not prone to. There is a vast deal of fun in it—plenty of good jokes,—but better than that, there is a force and delicacy of mental diagnosis (to speak professionally) that really surprised me. Carlyle & Emerson for instance—the distinctions are subtle enough for Duns Scotus, yet not fantastic. I thought I could see meaning in every little scintilla of a trait you pointed out; but it would have been a blank had not that wonderful comet-seeker of yours—your fine achromatic apprehension—directed my poor intellectual lenses to it.[11]

Lowell always had the ability—relatively rare—to judge himself accurately. In the "Fable" he writes:

> There is Lowell, who's striving Parnassus to climb
> With a whole bale of *isms* tied together with rhymes,
> He might get on alone, spite of brambles and boulders,

> But he can't with that bundle he has on his shoulders,
> The top of the hill he will ne'er come near reaching
> Till he learns the distinction 'twixt singing and preaching;
> His lyre has some chords that would ring pretty well,
> But he'd rather by half make a drum of the shell,
> And rattle away till he's old as Methusalem,
> At the head of a march to the last new Jerusalem.[12]

He voiced a similar self-criticism when he wrote some years later: "I shall never be a poet, until I get out of the pulpit, and New England was all meeting-house when I was growing up."[13]

The lack of taste that Lowell decried in Poe he also found obnoxious in Whitman, Swinburne, and in the letters of Jane Welch Carlyle. Among the comments that he made to Charles Norton on Whitman's *Leaves of Grass* was: "When a man aims at originality he acknowledges himself consciously unoriginal."[14] He thought Whitman's book had a superficial originality, loose technique, and untutored flamboyance; he also thought that Whitman overstepped bounds of moral propriety, and that his poems contained "downright animality." This last characteristic was also true of Swinburne. "I have not," he wrote to E. C. Stedman (Elmwood, Nov. 26, 1866), "seen Swinburne's new volume— but a poem or two from it which I have seen shocked me, and I am not squeamish." He goes on to say that for him unchastity of mind is worse than that of body: "Why should a man by choice go down to live in his cellar, instead of mounting to those fair upper chambers which look toward the sunrise of that Easter which shall greet the resurrection of the soul from the body of this death? . . . let no man write a line that he would not have his daughter read. When a man begins to lust after the Muse instead of loving her, he may be sure that it is never the Muse that he embraces."[15]

Mrs. Carlyle's *Correspondence* he called—in a letter to Norton from England, April 22, 1883—"a very painful book in more ways than one. There are disclosures there that never should have been made, as if they had been caught up from the babblings of discharged housemaids. One blushes in reading, and feels like a person caught listening at the keyhole. . . ."[16]

I *Prose Criticism*

Prose criticism appears throughout the letters, in the lecture series given at the Lowell Institute, and in the several volumes of essays—*My Study Windows,* the two volumes of *Among My Books,* and *Latest Literary Essays,* published posthumously. In these works, both the faults and the virtues of Lowell as writer, as well as critic, are manifested. The seemingly boundless wealth of his reading proved both fault and virtue. It could never be said that he was poorly equipped with knowledge of the subject of these essays. On the other hand, the vastness of his erudition tempted him into numerous digressions. A particular phase of Lowell's background that could "clutter" the subject of a paper was his extensive mastery of language. In itself, this is surely an attribute to any writer.

But the perfect essayist should not, as it were, select the choice word in the presence of his reader. Lowell even has the editor's pencil in hand as he quotes Dryden: "I am satisfied if it [rhyme] cause delight, for delight is the chief if not the only end of poesy [Lowell inserts "he should have said *means*"]; instruction can be admitted but in the second place, for poesy only instructs as it delights. . . ."[17] The essay on Dryden, that on Walton, and parts of *Shakespeare Once More* represent Lowell the prose critic at his best. It is difficult to find critical estimates of the first two writers that equal, much less exceed, Lowell's. Though the one on Shapespeare is episodic to a considerable degree, it compasses the immense scope of his genius.

We should demand for a perfect editor, then, first, a thorough glossological knowledge of the English contemporary with Shakespeare; second, enough logical acuteness of mind and metaphysical training to enable him to follow recondite processes of thought; third, such a conviction of the supremacy of his author as always to prefer his thought to any theory of his own; fourth, a feeling for music, and so much knowledge of the practice of other poets as to understand that Shakespeare's versification differs from theirs as often in kind as in degree; fifth, an acquaintance with the world as well as with books; and last, what is, perhaps, of more importance than all, so great a familiarity with the working of the imaginative faculty in general, and of its peculiar operation in the mind of Shakespeare, as will prevent his thinking a passage dark with excess of light, and enable him to understand fully that the Gothic Shakespeare often superimposed upon the slender column of a single word, that seems to twist under it, but does not,—like the quaint shafts in cloisters,—a weight of meaning which the modern architects of sentences would consider wholly unjustifiable by correct principle.[18]

One may disagree heartily with Lowell's interpretation of Hamlet's character or with his particular finding of allegory in *The Tempest,* but the greater part of his estimate of Shakespeare's genius is worth fuller consideration than is usually accorded it.

The Dryden and the Walton essays are—as has already been noted—superior to the others. Lowell, perhaps the most distinguished Man of Letters in America in the nineteenth century, presents Dryden, England's most distinguished Man of Letters in the seventeenth century, fairly and with discernment. The only façade of Dryden's many-sided genius that eluded Lowell is the poet's potentiality for lyric verse, so rarely manifested, but so superb in the two odes to Saint Cecilia. It has been generally conceded that, for the most part, one *admires* John Dryden; but, in the odes, one can *love* him. Lowell himself thought highly of this essay. He wrote in a letter to Mrs. Herrick, on August 5, 1875: ". . . I was pleased to find that you had read my essay on Dryden oftener than any other, for I believe it to be my best."[19]

Few men have written a single book such as Walton's *Compleat Angler* that has held the interest of the reading public uninterruptedly for upwards of three centuries, as Walton's volume has. Yet, few readers bother to inform themselves concerning its author. Lowell's essay, which was printed in the posthumous series, *Latest Literary Essays,* was a full consideration of Walton's importance, his personality, his style. In it he gave Walton's short biographies the recognition they had long lacked. For it was Isaak Walton who made contemporary biography significant. The idea that no person was a suitable subject for biographical study until he had been dead at least a half century was

shattered in these charming, intimate presentations of the
Reverend Robert Sanderson, John Donne, George Herbert, and
others.

Of Walton's style, Lowell says aptly:

> Walton, at any rate, in course of time, attained at least in
> prose, to something which, if it may not be called style, was a
> very charming way of writing, all the more so that he has an
> innocent air of not knowing how it is done. Natural endowment
> and predisposition may count for nine in ten of the chances of
> success in this competition, but no man ever achieved, as Walton
> sometimes did, a simplicity which leaves criticism helpless, by
> the mere light of nature alone. . . . Simplicity, when it is not a
> careless gift of the Muse, is the last and most painful achieve-
> ment of conscientious self-denial. He seems also to have had the
> true literary memory, which stores up the apt or pleasing word
> for use on occasion.[20]

As an example, he cites Walton's use of Donne's "elemented" as
a verb.

In commenting on Walton's "Elegy on Donne," he writes as
part of an excellent passage too long to quote in full:

> Yet now and then in the far inferior verse of far inferior men
> there will be some difficult word with a sob in it that moves as
> no artifice can move, and brings back to each of us his private
> loss with a strange sense of comfort in feeling that somewhere,
> no matter how far away in the past, there was one who had
> suffered like ourselves and would not be appeased by setting his
> pain to music. There is something of this in Walton's "Elegy on
> Donne."[21]

I think that Walton's prose owes much to the poetic sentiment
in him which was denied a refuge in verse, and that his practice
in metres may have given to his happier periods a measure and
a music they would otherwise have wanted.[22]

Lowell articulates perfectly the reader's enchantment with the
naturalness of Walton's presentation of episodes, such as his
meeting with Sanderson near *Little Britain* where Sanderson had
been to buy a book. When sudden wind and rain drive them into
a "cleanly house where we had bread, cheese, ale, and a fire

for our money," the reader spends the hour with them. It is, Lowell puts it, "exactly as if he were telling us of it, and this sweet persuasiveness of the living and naturally cadenced voice is never wanting in Walton. It is indeed his distinction, and it is a very rare quality in writers, upon most of whom, if they ever happily forget themselves and fall into the tone of talk, the pen too soon comes spluttering in."[23]

Those who have only adverse opinion of Lowell as critic—such as Joseph J. Reilly in a volume on Lowell in that role and Van Wyck Brooks in shorter allusions to this aspect of Lowell in *The Flowering of New England*—have failed to find the gold amid the dross. Charles Sumner wrote Longfellow from Washington, on February 6, 1855: "Lowell's lecture on Milton lifted me for a whole day. It was the utterance of genius in honor of genius.[24]

In the conclusion of the chapter on Lowell in *Old Cambridge,* Thomas Wentworth Higginson wrote: ". . . not always judicial in criticism, especially in early years, yet steadily expanding and deepening. . . ."[25] Edward Everett Hale, in *James Russell Lowell and His Friends,* has this to say: "One of the men of letters whose impressions of such a life every one is glad to read writes to me of Lowell's work: 'Mr. Lowell excelled at once in original and critical work, thus giving the lie to the sneer that a critic is a person who has failed as a creator.'"[26] And finally, there is a comment from William Dean Howells: ". . . in his lectures on the English poets, given not many years before he came to the charge of the *Atlantic,* he had proved himself easily the wisest and finest critic in our language."[27]

CHAPTER 6

Professor and Mentor

"... the most inspiring teacher."[1]

FOR NEARLY TWENTY YEARS, Lowell functioned as a professor at Harvard. Essentially this position reduced the amount of creative work produced during these years. He did, however, something of great significance at this time: he shared his vast erudition and enthusiasm for Dante and Calderon, as well as for English and American writers, with the eager minds of Harvard undergraduates through his lectures, and with his closest friends through his letters. Nor were these completely arid years in his poetry and prose. To them belong the second Biglow series, the "Commemoration Ode" and many maturer poems, as well as a generous sprinkling of forceful articles. If Harvard students of those twenty years thought of Longfellow as a poet who had been a professor and of Lowell as a professor who had been a poet, these last-mentioned works must have jolted them into a realization that Professor Lowell was indeed still a very distinguished poet.

Something of the uniqueness of personality and independence of thought and approach marked Professor Lowell, just as they had marked the purely literary Lowell of earlier years. To appreciate as fully as possible the character of Lowell as professor and mentor, one must assemble opinions—those of Barrett Wendell (one of his most distinguished pupils and one who was in *his* turn to teach at Harvard)—and gather from the letters passages in which Lowell discoursed on literature as he must have done in the classroom.

When it became known that Longfellow was to resign from the Smith Professorship of the French and Spanish Languages and Literatures and the Professorship of Belles Lettres at Harvard, there were six candidates for the position, all of whom were friends of Longfellow. Lowell was not one of the six, but a series of lectures he had given at the Lowell Institute had been so successful that he was chosen for the post. Longfellow wrote in his diary for January 31, 1855: "I am sorry for some of my friends who want the place. But for lectures, I think Lowell the best of the candidates. He has won his spurs and will give the college just what it needs."[2]

Every professor has his favorite course; Lowell's was the course in Dante. Because of the small size of the classes, it was possible for him to meet his students in his own study in the house on Kirkland Street and to give that individual attention that is so desirable, but often impossible, in teaching. The richness of his own literary background, the graciousness of the man and his humor and understanding endeared him to the students, who must have remembered him as a rare person in their undergraduate experience. For all these endearing qualities, Lowell had before him the strict ideals of the true purpose of teaching: "I believe that the study of imaginative literature tends to sanity of mind, and to keep the Caliban of common sense, a very useful monster in his proper place, from making himself king over us. It is a study of order, proportion, arrangement, of the highest and purest Reason. It teaches that chance has less to do with success than forethought, will and work."[3]

I   Barrett Wendell's Impressions and Tributes

Barrett Wendell was a pupil in the Dante class during 1876 and 1877, Lowell's last two years of regular teaching. Wendell remembered his first impression of his professor as that of a man eccentric in appearance, "surprisingly hirsute," dressed in an old doublebreasted sack-coat, his tie in a sailor knot, adorned with a pin (an accessory then definitely out of fashion in the opinion of the young men students). He was famous for his silk hat which seemed always to need brushing. Even Mrs. Lowell objected to the plaid trousers that pleased his fancy. The word that came to Wendell's mind when he first went to ask the Professor's permission to enter the course was "quizzical." This odd, quizzical, somewhat eccentric man was to rate later in Wendell's opinion as "the most human instructor ever vouchsafed Harvard youth."

Commenting on the professor's approach to Dante, Wendell writes:

> Mr. Lowell never gave us less than a canto to read; and often gave us two or three. He never, from the beginning, bothered us with a particle of linguistic irrelevance. Here before us was a great poem—a lasting impression of what human life had meant to a human being, dead and gone these five centuries. Let us try, as best we might to see what life had meant to this man; let us see what relation his experiences, great and small, bore to ours; and, now and then, let us pause for a moment to notice how wonderfully beautiful his expression of this experience was. Let us read, as sympathetically as we could make ourselves read, the words of one who was as much a man as we, only vastly greater in his knowledge of wisdom and beauty. That was the spirit of Mr. Lowell's teaching. It opened to some of us a new world. In a month, I could read Dante better than I ever learned to read Greek, or Latin, or German.[4]

And Barrett Wendell had entered the course with no knowledge of Italian.

In an essay "Mr. Lowell as a Teacher," the seventh one in Wendell's volume *Stelligeri and Other Essays Concerning America*,[5] he tells of the open house that Lowell held for his students one evening a week at his home. He placed these young men so much at their ease that they would visit him on other evenings too. There they would find him, dressed in a smoking jacket and slippers, enjoying his pipe by the open fire. They were free to discourse on literature, or Lowell might talk at length in his urbane way, never letting them forget, for example, that Dante was a human being, just as they were. As in the classroom they "gave up notebooks in a week," in the master's study they also sat enthralled.

Lowell found the mechanical details of teaching more than distasteful. He would be long in returning examination papers. When a student once inquired about them, Lowell asked what he thought he deserved. The student said he hoped he had merited 60 per cent. Lowell allegedly replied: "You may take it, and I shan't have the bother of reading your book."[6]

Wendell, who availed himself often of the privileged visits to Elmwood, recalls that one evening, when he was the sole visitor, Lowell had just lost a dear friend. He spoke so beautifully of death that Wendell was moved to write: "That talk was such a poem as I have never read."[7] As graduation time approached for Wendell's class, the dissensions over senior elections brought a ruling that denied the group its traditional Class Day festivities. Though Lowell was shortly leaving for his assignment as minister at Madrid, he invited the class to an open-air breakfast at Elmwood. It was not until his return from his English mission in 1885 that Wendell met Lowell again; and the former pupil was rather shocked to find that the professor whom he had admired so much had quite forgotten his face, and almost his name. Apparently Lowell's interest in these young men was as a group of students, not as individuals.

That his twenty years as professor had meant much to Lowell, however, is brought out in connection with the dinner that was given to him at the Tavern Club on his seventieth birthday. In the various speeches of tribute, no mention was made of Lowell as a teacher. Wendell, who was present, resented the omission; and, speaking to the guest of honor afterward, he told Lowell that he would always be to him the most inspiring teacher he ever had. Lowell replied: "I'm glad you said that. I've been wondering if I hadn't wasted half my life."[8]

In an unpublished lecture, Lowell chose Dante as the text for a discourse on how to read great literature. He said:

One is sometimes asked by young men to recommend to them a course of reading. My advice would always be to confine yourself to the supreme books in whatever literature; still better, to choose some one great author and grow thoroughly familiar with him. For as all roads lead to Rome, so they also lead thence;

and you will find that in order to understand perfectly and weigh exactly any really vital piece of literature, you will be gradually and pleasantly persuaded to studies and explorations of which you little dreamed when you began, and will find yourselves scholars before you are aware. If I may be allowed a personal illustration, it was my own profound admiration for the "Divina Commedia" of Dante that lured me into what little learning I possess. For remember that there is nothing less fruitful than scholarship for the sake of mere Scholarship, nor anything more wearisome in the attainment. But the moment you have an object and a centre, attention is quickened, the mother of memory; and whatever you acquire groups and arranges itself in an order which is lucid because it is everywhere in intelligent relation to an object of constant and growing interest. Thus, as respects Dante, I asked myself, What are his points of likeness or unlikeness with the authors of classical antiquity? in how far is either of these an advantage or defect? What and how much modern literature had preceded him? How much was he indebted to it? How far had the Italian language been subdued and sup pled to the uses of poetry or prose before his time? How much did he color the style or thought of the authors who followed him? Is it a fault or a merit that he is so thoroughly impregnated with the opinions, passions, and even prejudices not only of his age but his country? Was he right or wrong in being a Ghibelline? To what extent is a certain freedom of opinion which he shows sometimes on points of religious doctrine to be attributed to the humanizing influences of the Crusades in enlarg ing the horizon of the Western mind by bringing it in contact with other races, religions, and social arrangements? These and a hundred other such questions were constant stimulants to thought and inquiry, stimulants such as no merely objectless and, so to speak, impersonal study could have supplied.[9]

II *Mentor and Critic in the Letters*

Choice comment on a variety of writers, which appeared in letters during the years of his professorship, suggest the sort of comments in class that must have alerted the interest of students so that, as Wendell expressed it, notebooks were put aside in a week.

To Norton, he wrote on August 1, 1864:

> I have read Boccaccio nearly through since Commencement—
> I mean the "Decameron," in order to appreciate his style. I find
> it very charming, and him clearly the founder of modern prose.
> A singular sweetness, ease, and grace. Nothing came near it for
> centuries. And then the just visible unobtrusive play of humor—
> a kind of heat-lightning round the horizon of his mind without
> a harmful bolt in the whole of it. And then there is no great
> mischief in his dirt. When Casti versifies his stories you feel this—
> for Casti makes them bad. . . .[10]

In a letter to Thayer from London, December 24, 1883, he
made this observation on the poetry of Emerson: "As for Emerson's verse (though he has written some as exquisite as any in
the language) I suppose we must give it up. That he had a
sense of the higher harmonies of language no one that ever heard
him lecture can doubt. The structure of his prose, as one
listened to it, was as nobly metrical as the King James version
of the Old Testament, and this made it all the more puzzling
that he should have been absolutely insensitive to the harmony
of verse."[11]

As a scholar Lowell belonged to the group possessed of a
rich, broad familiarity with many fields of literature and even
other arts. He was the Renaissance scholar rather than the
scientific, German one who was meticulously informed in a
narrow field and knew no greater satisfaction than that of having many footnotes on every page of his writing. Lowell was a
humanist *par excellence*.

> Human, after all, [Wendell wrote] is the word which most
> often recurs as one tries to phrase what Lowell means; and
> "human" is an adjective which applies equally to two distinctly
> different nouns. In one sense the most truly human being is he
> who most strives to understand those records of the past to
> which we give the name of the humanities. In another sense the
> most deeply human being is he who strives most to understand
> the humanity about him. It was unceasing effort to fuse his
> understanding of the humanities with his understanding of
> humanity which made Lowell so often seem paradoxical.[12]

[76]

Lowell's keen critical intuitiveness made it possible for him to make cogent judgments on the great writers of both English and continental literatures, as well as on contemporary Americans in the "Fable for Critics." The superb judgments are sometimes entangled in pages of diffuse writing or digressions that make the reader think less of complete essays than of matchless bits. But Lowell always returns from digressions to the main path of thought, and the digressions are often priceless in themselves. He gained considerable importance indeed in the field of philological and linguistic scholarship. Here, again, if not meticulously accurate in the matter of word derivations, he more than makes up for his lack by a remarkable verbal memory, a familiarity with the actual *use* of words in half a dozen languages, plus a poet's sense of word values. His paper called "Library of Old Authors" demonstrates this admirably, as does the introduction to the *Biglow Papers, Second Series.*

In a lecture on "The First Need of American Culture," printed in part in the Harvard *Crimson* (May 4, 1894), he said: "True scholarship consists in knowing not what things exist, but what they mean; it is not memory but judgment. It is the foundation of true criticism. And the advantage of a proper cultivation of the critical faculty is that it helps us to composure, to self-possession, those things above all others desirable."

Many of the choicest comments about literature are in his letters to Charles Norton:

> What an extraordinary threefold nature that was of Dante's! The more you study him the more sides you find, and yet the ray from him is always white light. I learn continually to prize him more as man, poet, artist, moralist, and teacher. Without him there were no Italy. And the Italian commentators forever twitching at his sleeve and trying to make him say he is of their way of thinking! Of their way, indeed! One would think he might be free of them, at least, in Paradise. He becomes daily more clear and more mysterious to me. What a web a man can spin out of his life if a man be only a genius! . . .[13]

Again, he wrote to Norton on June 13, 1858: "My notion of a true lyric is that the meaning should float steadfast in the centre of every stanza, while the vapory emotions (protean in

form as you will) float up to it and over it, and wreathe it with
an opal halo which seems their own, but is truly its own work.
The shades of emotion over, there floats the meaning, clear and
sole and sharp-cut in its own luminous integrity."[14]

On Keats he wrote to Charles Briggs that he was ". . . a rare
and great genius. He had, I think, the finest and richest fancy
that has been seen since Shakespeare. And his imagination gave
promise of an equal development. Ought we to sorrow for his
early death, or to be glad that we have in his works an eternal
dawn of poesy, as in Shakespeare we have early morning and
full day? Forever and forever shall we be able to bathe our
temples in the cool dew which hangs upon his verse."[15]

Lowell makes a neat distinction between humor and wit in a
letter to Briggs, November 13, 1847:

> . . . Perhaps I can explain what I mean by humor if I say
> (and I am sure you will agree with me in it) that Fielding has
> vastly more *conception* of humor than Dickens, and Dickens
> vastly more *observation* of humor than Fielding. Dickens seems
> to me for the most part to be rather a sketcher of humoristic
> characters (characters in themselves humorous and as such noted
> by him) than himself a humorist. My idea of the distinction be-
> tween wit and humor is that wit makes others laugh, and humor
> ourselves cry sometimes. Waldo Emerson is an amusing instance
> of a . . . man who is keenly alive to the incongruousness of
> *things* but has no perception (or little) of ludicrous *ideas*.[16]

Few students nodded in Lowell's classes. There was always
the excitement, as Barrett Wendell says, of not knowing what
this professor would do or say next. Who knows how many
aspiring young litterateurs either confidently or shyly showed
their manuscripts to Professor Lowell. For example, Lowell one
time advised the young Howells: "Don't print too much and too
soon; don't get married in a hurry; read what will make you
think, not *dream;* hold yourself dear; and more power to your
elbow! God bless you!"[17]

In a letter to Norton from Florence, February 2, 1874, Lowell
comments on himself as a professor:

I was never good for much as a professor—once a week, perhaps, at the best, when I could manage to get some conceit of
myself, and so could put a *little* of my *go* into the boys. The rest
of the time my desk was as good as I. And then, on the other
hand, my being professor wasn't good for me—it damped my
gunpowder, as it were, and my mind, when it took fire at all
(which wasn't often), drawled off in an unwilling fuse instead
of leaping to meet the first spark. . . .[18]

How regrettable it is that the notebooks were put aside in a
week, or that tape-recorders came too late. If the literal-minded
students relaxed in the classes where a lesson plan was followed
dutifully, other, perhaps better young minds opened up gloriously
as they listened to the "rhapsodies" of Professor Lowell.

CHAPTER 7

Political Writings

"... solely with the hope of doing good."[1]

THE PENDULUM of Lowell's temperament swung between the two extremes of the dreamer and the reformer, not to ultimate limits in either direction, but on the whole evenly. The idealist, the man of delicate sensitivity, the man of imagination, even of vision, is easy to find in Lowell, the reformer, the man who feels deeply for the oppressed, deeply enough to articulate his feelings, is surprising to find in a man of his background and in his day. Yet, this second man was as real as the first. Many accounts of him imply that it was Maria White who stirred his interests in this direction. There is no doubt that she nurtured and strengthened his human feeling, but the instincts were there to be fostered. He actually *inherited* a feeling for Abolitionism. His grandfather, John Lowell, was the one who introduced the clause abolishing slavery in Massachusetts into the Bill of Rights.[2] Younger than Whittier and Longfellow, whose anti-slavery poems are equally effective opposites of realism and romanticism, respectively, Lowell's first poems on the subject are insignificant when compared with either group. It was rather the very fact that James Russell Lowell was lending his interest and talents to the antislavery publications that helped and encouraged the cause.

In a letter to Tom Hughes, Lowell stated that when he wrote the *First Series* of *Biglow Papers* he believed that the war with Mexico (though the United States had just grounds) was essentially a war of false pretenses, and that it would result in widening the boundaries and thus prolonging the life of slavery.

"Leaving the sin of it to God, I believed and still believe that slavery is the Achilles heel of our polity; that it is a temporary and false supremacy of the white races, sure to destroy that supremacy at last, because an enslaved people always prove themselves of more enduring fibre than their enslavers, as not suffering from the social vices sure to be engendered by oppression in the governing class."[3] He thought all men should protest this situation.

The most quoted lines—"What Mr. Robinson thinks"—were written at a single sitting; in fact, much of the writing was done rapidly. Lowell said that he conceived the character of Parson Wilbur "with his pedantry and verbosity, his amiable vanity and superiority to the verses he was editing, as a fitting artistic background and foil,"[4] when he came to collect and publish the papers in a volume. He regretted the exaggerated bad spelling he had used for Hosea at first and wrote C. F. Briggs:

> As for Hosea, I am sorry that I began making him such a detestable speller. There is no fun in bad spelling of itself, but only where the misspelling suggests something else which is droll *per se*. You see I am getting him out of it gradually. I mean to altogether. Parson Wilbur is about to propose a subscription for fitting him for college, and has already commenced his education. Perhaps you like the last best because it is more personal and has therefore more directness of purpose. But I confess I think that Birdofredom's attempt to explain the Anglo-Saxon theory is the best thing yet, except Parson Wilbur's letter in the *Courier* of last Saturday (today week). The only further use I shall put Hosea to will be to stir up the Legislater at the next session on the subject of allowing women to retain their own earnings, etc.[5]

I *First Series of* Biglow Papers

There were nine *Biglow Papers* in the First Series. Number I consists of a letter from Ezekiel Biglow (Hosea's father) to the Honorable Joseph T. Buckingham, editor of the *Boston Courier*. The father explains how Hosea met a recruiting sergeant in Boston who tried to get Hosea to join up for service in the Mexican War. Hosea wrote his poem of protest that night, and the father enclosed it in his letter to the editor. Perhaps its best known stanza is the fifth:

> Ez fer war, I call it murder,—
>   There you hev it plain an' flat;
> I don't want to go no furder
>   Than my Testyment fer that;
> God hez sed so plump an' fairly,
>   It's ez long ez it is broad
> An' you've gut to git up airly
>   Ef you want to take in God.⁶

The Reverend Homer Wilbur appended a brief note to this poem.

Number II starts with a letter of Hosea's to the *Courier's* editor covering a letter from Birdofredum Sawin, a private in the Massachusetts regiment. Hosea's letter is preceded by Parson Wilbur's note on the use of verse as a natural mode of expression. Hosea has put Sawin's prose into verse. Birdofredum is fully enlisted and finds his position detestable. This number ends with a long anti-Papist note by Parson Wilbur.

A satire on the "pernicious sentiment" in "Our country right or wrong" distinguishes Number III, probably the best known of this series. Caleb is Colonel Cushing of Newburyport, Colonel of the Massachusetts Regiment of Volunteers; Guvener B is George Nixon Briggs, the Whig Governor of Massachusetts from 1844-57. Colonel Cushing was later raised by President Polk to the rank of Brigadier-General. He was upheld in the campaign of 1847 by John Paul Robinson, who shifted from zealous support of the Whigs to the side of the Democrats:

> The side of our country must ollers be took,
>   An' President Polk, you know, *he* is our country
> An' the angel thet writes all our sins in a book
>   Puts the *debit* to *him*, an' to us the *per contry;*
>   An' John P.
>   Robinson he
> Sez this is his view o' the thing to a T.⁷

Number IV features Hosea's verse report of the speech delivered by Increase D. O'Phace, Esquire, on Mr. John Gorham Palfrey's refusal to vote for Mr. R. C. Winthrop, the Whig candidate for Speaker of the House in the Thirtieth Congress. Mr. Winthrop was elected after three ballots. Mr. Palfrey's reason for his refusal was a conviction that Mr. Winthrop would not use his influence to stop the war and to prevent the extension of slavery to the new territory. Parson Wilbur's long, detailed observations both before and after the rhymed addresses or letters contain many pithy bits on truth, faculties of speech, etc., but also many dry passages.

The title of No. V is "The Debate in the Sennit, Sot to a Nusry Rhyme." It is a satire on the stir created by the attempt of Captain Drayton and his mate Sayers to abduct seventy-seven slaves from Washington in the schooner *Pearl*. The slaves were recaptured and sold South. The District Court convicted and sentenced Drayton and Sayers to long terms in prison, but in 1852 an unconditional pardon was granted by President Fillmore through the interest of Senator Sumner. When Senator John Hale of New Hampshire introduced to Congress a resolution implying sympathy with the slaves, the slave-holders were roused to wrath. Calhoun attacked Senator Hale violently. This section is written in a stanza pattern similar to the John P. Robinson letter.

A different stanza is used for No. VI, "The Pious Editor's Creed," the editor being he of the *Jaalam Independent Blunderbuss*. Parson Wilbur says in his notes: ". . . I would derive the name of *editor* not so much from *edo*, to publish, as from *edo*, to eat, that being the peculiar profession to which he esteems himself called. He blows up the flames of political discord for no other occasion than that he may thereby handily boil his own pot. I believe there are two thousand of these mutton-loving shepherds in the United States, and of these, how many have even the dimmest perception of their immense power, and the duties consequent thereon? Here and there, haply, one. Nine hundred and ninety-nine labor to impress upon the people the great principles of *Tweedledum,* and other nine hundred and ninety-nine preach with equal earnestness the gospel according to *Tweedledee*." The last two stanzas of the Creed are as follows:

> I du believe wutever trash
> 'll keep the people in blindness,—

> Thet we the Mexicans can thrash
>   Right inter brotherly kindness,
> Thet bombshells, grape, an' powder 'n' ball
>   Air good-will's strongest magnets,
> Thet peace, to make it stick at all,
>   Must be driv in with bagnets.
>
> In short, I firmly du believe
>   In Humbug generally,
> Fer it's a thing thet I perceive
>   To hev a solid vally;
> This heth my faithful shepherd ben,
>   In pasturs sweet heth led me,
> An' this'll keep the people green
>   To feed ez they hev fed me.[8]

Number VII is a letter "from a candidate for the presidency in answer to suttin questions proposed by Mr. Hosea Biglow, inclosed in a note from Mr. Biglow to S. H. Gay, Esq., Editor of the *National Anti-Slavery Standard.*" This paper opens with Homer Wilbur's views on curiosity as the quality which preeminently distinguishes and segregates man from the lower animals and then continues with a discourse on letters of various types. Hosea's rhymed letter is a parody on the shifting loyalties of Zachary Taylor:

> Ez to my princerples, I glory
>   In hevin' nothin' o' the sort;
> I ain't a Wig, I ain't a Tory,
>   I'm just a canderdate, in short;
> Thet's fair an' square an' parpendicler
>   But, ef the Public care a fig
> To hev me an'thin' in particler
>   Wy, I'm a kind o' peri-Wig.[9]

A second letter from B. Sawin, Esq. is the central interest in Number VIII. Birdofredum is back from the war, minus one leg, one eye, and one arm. He contemplates his chances of running for president, but he realizes that one must hail from the South to be considered for that office.

The last of Lowell's first *Biglow Papers* is Number IX., "A Third Letter from B. Sawin, Esq." In this missive, Birdofredum is stating his opinions of Whigs and Democrats:

I've been a Wig three weeks myself, jest o' this mod'rate sort,
An' don't find them an' Demmercrats so defferent ez I thought;
They both act pooty much alike, an' push an' scrouge an' cus;
They're like two pickpockets in league fer Uncle Samwell's pus;
Each takes a side, an' then they squeeze the ole man in be-
    tween 'em,
Turn all his pockets wrong side out an' quick ez lightnin'
    clean 'em;
To nary one on em I'd trust a secon' handed rail
No furder off'an I could sling a bullock by the tail.[10]

Ferris Greenslet has expressed especially well the qualities of this letter:

. . . if we look below the delightful Peacockian prose of the old man and beneath the Yankee garb of Hosea, we shall find that the characters dramatize the two chief sides of Lowell himself even more perfectly than they do two major strains of the New England character. Lowell never outgrew the vernacular wit and wisdom of Hosea, any more than he ever ceased to partake of that old-world lore of Parson Wilbur, which is bodied forth in such full-cadenced prose. . . . he never expressed his very self more characteristically than in the rhyming of Jaalam's bard, and in the concerted paragraphs of her Dominie."[11]

A pirated edition of the *Biglow Papers*, printed by Trübner & Co., was issued in England in 1859; and an authorized edition appeared shortly afterward, prefaced by Lowell's good friend in his later days, Thomas Hughes. The kernel of his judgment, tersely presented, is in the following paragraph:

Greece had her Aristophanes; Rome her Juvenal; Spain had her Cervantes; France her Rabelais, her Molière, her Voltaire; Germany her Jean Paul, her Heine; England her Swift, her Thackeray; and America has her Lowell. By the side of great masters of satire, though kept somewhat in the rear by provincialism of style, and subject, the author of the "Biglow Papers" holds his own place distinct from each and all. The man who reads the book for the first time, and is capable of understanding it, has received a new sensation. In Lowell the American mind has for the first time flowered out into thoroughly original genius.[12]

II Biglow Papers, *Second Series*

A considerable number of years separated the First and Second *Biglow Papers*. When Lowell was asked by J. T. Fields as the *Atlantic* editor to procure more of Hosea's poems from Parson Wilbur—numbers of Lowell's friends had also urged this continuation—he expressed a wish that the poems would "make him write them" as they had before. It is understandable that this kind of "character writing" must be spontaneous or fail.

The occasion of the later series was more important than that of the first, and the writing reflects the difference. It is also clearly the writing of a deeper thinking and vastly more experienced poet. For all that, Lowell found it difficult to return to the genre of this work. He ended a letter to Fields on January 1, 1862: "Good-by-yours—with a series of Biglows rising like the visionary kings before Macbeth, to destroy all present satisfaction."[13]

The first of the new series appeared in January 1862. The needed stimulus came in the *Trent* affair which inspired "Mason and Slidell; a Yankee Idyll," which was printed in February. "If I am not mistaken," Lowell wrote to Fields, "it will *take*." The third, fourth, fifth, and sixth followed in monthly succession, March through June. Then Lowell's rustic muse failed him. On June 5, he wrote Fields that he had reached an impasse: "It's no use. I reverse that gospel difficulty and while the flesh is willing enough, the spirit is weak. My brain must be fallow a spell— there is no super-phosphate for those worn-out fields. Better no crop than small potatoes. I want to have the passion of the thing on me again and beget lusty Biglows."[14]

After the lapse of a half-year, the "Latest Views of Mr. Biglow" appeared in February 1863; "Mr. Hosea Biglow to the Editor of the *Atlantic*" in April 1865, and the final one, "Mr. Hosea Biglow's Speech in March Meeting" in May 1866. In the autumn of 1866 the entire Second Series was published, somewhat amplified, in book form.

Lowell reverted to his former plan to put Parson Wilbur to death and made the seventh paper "Latest Views of Mr. Biglow," published in the February 1863 *Atlantic*. Other things absorbed his attention, with the result that no more papers appeared until the moving tenth satire published in April 1865. The final paper, called out by the Johnson retrograde movement, was printed in May 1866. Numbers VIII and IX did not appear until the complete book was published later that year. The volume was inscribed to E. R. Hoar.

Although the second *Biglow Papers* may lack some of the youthful zest of the earlier set, they are in no sense a "less successful sequel" to an earlier work. The gains are greater than any possible losses. Charles Norton regarded Lowell's writings during the years of the Rebellion as "among the most powerful and effective of the sentiment and opinions of the North."[15] Lowell's effectiveness as delegate and afterwards presidential elector at Cincinnati in 1876 drew special attention.

The best introduction to the Second Series is found in Lowell's prose papers contributed to the *Atlantic Monthly* and the *North American Review* from 1858-1860, some of which have been reprinted in the fifth volume of the Riverside edition of his writings. Just before Mr. Lincoln's election in 1860, Lowell wrote: "We are approaching a crisis in our domestic policy more momentous than any that has arisen since we became a nation." The crisis arrived; and during 1861 his political sagacity, his ardent patriotism, and his moral genius were displayed in a series of essays which did much to enlighten and confirm the roused spirit of the Northern people. But more was wanting of him. His verse could reach more ears than his or any other writer's prose.

Once the spirit of the *Biglow Papers* was revived, Lowell seemed even more prolific and more keenly witty in the Second Series. He wrote Longfellow in 1866 that he had been working on an Introduction on Yankeeisms to that series that had grown to some sixty printed pages. This long preface is in the appendix to the Cambridge edition of the complete poems. In it he explains his approach and the characters in a way which clarifies what would at times be baffling interweaving of *leitmotifs.* Hosea Biglow was a type of "up-country" man such as the poet had often seen at anti-slavery meetings. The Reverend Mr. Wilbur was created to "express the more cautious element of the New England character and its pedantry," one who could complement Hosea. Birdofredum Sawin was to fulfill the character of clown with his droll observations. He proved the "incarnation . . . of national recklessness as to right and wrong. . . ."[16] Of his choice of the Yankee dialect writing, Lowell said:

In choosing the Yankee dialect, I did not act without forethought. It had long seemed to me that the great vice of American writing and speaking was a studied want of simplicity, that we were coming to look on our mother-tongue as a dead language, to be sought in the grammar and dictionary rather than in the heart, and that our only chance of escape was by seeking it at its living sources among those who were, as Scottowe says of Major-General Gibbons, "divinely illiterate." . . . It is only from its roots in the living generations of men that a language can be reinforced with fresh vigor for its needs; what may be called a literate dialect grows ever more and more pedantic and foreign, till it becomes at last as unfitting a vehicle for living thought as monkish Latin. That we should all be made to talk like books is the danger with which we are threatened by the Universal Schoolmaster, who does his best to enslave the minds and memories of his victims to what he esteems the best models of English composition, that is to say, to the writers whose style is faultily correct and has no blood-warmth in it. . . .[17]

He gives copious and interesting examples of so-called vulgarisms that stem from aristocratic English ancestry. The introduction to the First Series contains the general rules for Yankee pronunciation, using as an example a Yankeeized version of Richard III's speech "Now is the winter of our discontent." At the time the Introduction to the first series was going through the press, the editor asked Lowell for something to fill up a vacant page. For this need, the poet improvised an extract from a supposed ballad of Mr. Biglow's. The printer cut it off when the space was filled. When readers begged for the rest of it, Lowell completed it and revised it, adding further characterization and making it into a connected story. In this completed form, "The Courtin' " was placed at the end of the Introduction to Series Two. It turned out to be an enchanting pastoral that has never lost the immediate popularity it won when first printed.

The editors of the *Atlantic* saw fit to curtail Parson Wilbur's long introductory prose letter to Number I. It is actually cut off in mid-sentence. The dialect verse letter is from Birdofredum Sawin, Esq., to Hosea. He writes of being tarred and feathered on a false conviction of robbery, and then of his marriage to a southern widow, The Widder Shennon.

Number II is one of the masterpieces of the series: "Mason and Slidell; a Yankee Idyll." Mason of Virginia and Slidell of Louisiana were sent by President Davis at the end of 1861 as agents to represent the Southern cause in England and France. They eluded the blockade of Charleston harbor, landed at Havana, and embarked for St. Thomas on the British mail steamer *Trent*. On the way, Captain Wilkes of the American man-of-war *San Jacinto* stopped the *Trent* and took Mason and Slidell prisoners. Though the prisoners were released on the demand of Lord Russell, a hostile feeling continued between England and the North. Lowell's famous debate between Concord Bridge and Bunker Hill Monument discusses the attitude of England in some detail. The section ends pleasantly yet pointedly with the ballad-like "Jonathan to John," concluding:

> Shall it be love, or hate, John?
>   It's you thet's to decide;
> Ain't your bonds held by Fate John,
>   Like all the world's beside?
>   Ole Uncle S. sez he, "I guess
>   Wise men forgive," sez he,
> But not forgit; an some time yit
>   Thet truth may strike J.B.,
>   Ez well ez you an' me!

> God means to make this land, John,
>   Clear thru, from sea to sea,
> Believe an' understand, John,
>   The *wuth* o' bein free.
>   Ole Uncle S. sez he, "I guess,
>   God's price is high," sez he;
> But nothin' else than wut He sells
>   Wears long, an' thet J.B.
> May larn, like you an' me![18]

Parson Wilbur's letter that opens Number III is dated "Jaalam, 7th Feb., 1862." Enclosed in it is a letter of Birdofredum to Mr. Hosea telling how he was converted at a Southern camp meeting and therefore finally married to the widow who would not have him without religion. Most of the letter explains his sympathies with the Southern cause.

Number IV, "A Message of Jeff Davis in Secret Session Conjecturally reported by H. Biglow," is enclosed in the usual letter of Homer Wilbur to the editors. In his letter he states succinctly Lowell's view of emancipation:

> I think that nothing will ever give permanent peace and security to this continent but the extirpation of Slavery therefrom, and that the occasion is nigh; but I would do nothing hastily or vindictively, nor presume to jog the elbow of Providence. . . . To make Emancipation a reform instead of a revolution is worth a little patience, that we may have the Border States first, and then the non-slaveholders of the Cotton States, with us in principle,—a consummation that seems to be nearer than many imagine. . . . Our first duty toward our enslaved brother is to educate him, whether he be white or black. The first need of the free black is to elevate himself according to the standard of this material generation. So soon as the Ethiopian goes in his chariot, he will find not only Apostles, but Chief Priests and Scribes and Pharisees willing to ride with him.[19]

Biglow Number V contains the "Speech of Honourable Preserved Doe in Secret Caucus." The parson turns from the theme of War to write his introduction on a runic inscription. "Preserved Doe" airs his views on the confidence and loyalty of the people swinging from the South to the North. He concludes:

> . . . I guess "Abolition" 'll work a spell yit,
> When the war's done, an' so will "Forgive-an' forgit."
> Times mus' be pooty thoroughly outo' all jint,
> Ef we can't make a good constitootional pint;
> An' the good time'll come to be grindin' our exes,
> When the war goes to seed in the nettle o' texes;
> Ef Jon'than don't squirm, with sech helps to assist him,
> I give up my faith in the free-suffrage system;
> Democ'cy wun't be nut a mite interestin',
> Nor p'litikle capital much wuth investin';
> An' my notion is, to keep dark an' lay low
> Till we see the right minute to put in our blow."20

A delightfully refreshing mood pervades Number VI. "Sunthin' in the Pastoral Line." This paper for May 1862 opens with a very short introduction by the good Parson. Hosea's letter is redolent of approaching spring. The descriptive part culminates with these joyous lines:

> 'nuff sed, June's bridesman, poet o' the year,
> Gladness on wings, the bobolink, is here;
> Half-hid in tip-top apple-blooms he swings,
> Or climbs aginst the breeze with quiverin' wings,
> Or, givin' way to't in a mock despair,
> Runs down, a brook o' laughter, thru the air.21

Hosea walks to the deserted little one-story schoolhouse which floods his mind and heart with nostalgic memories until he sleeps. In a dream his "gret-gret-gret-gran'ther" appears and urges him to action rather than theory. "Chance wun't stop to listen to debatin'!"

> "Strike soon," sez he, "or you'll be deadly ailin',
> Folks thet's afeared to fail are sure o' failin';
> God hates your sneakin' creturs thet believe
> He'll settle things they run away an' leave!"
> He brought his foot down fercely, ez he spoke,
> An' give me sech a startle thet I woke.22

In Number VII, "Latest Views of Mr. Biglow," the editors of the *Atlantic* tell in a preliminary note of the death on Christmas Day, 1862, of the Reverend Homer Wilbur, A.M. This note also contains some tasteful, adulatory comments by his friend and colleague, Reverend Jeduthun Hitchcock. There was found on Parson Wilbur's desk a fragment of a letter obviously intended to accompany Mr. Biglow's contribution to the eighth letter. He expresses in it disagreement with Hosea's extreme views; he says cogently: "On the one hand there are those who do not see that the vital principle of Government and the seminal principle of Law cannot properly be made a subject of compromise at all, and on the other those who are equally blind to the truth that without a compromise of individual opinions, interests, and even rights, no society would be possible."[23] Hosea's verses urge support of the monitory Proclamation issued by President Lincoln on September 22, 1862, announcing that on the first day of the next year he would exercise his war-power and emancipate all slaves of those States, or parts of States, in rebellion which failed to comply with certain conditions.

Biglow VIII, "Kettelopotomachia" informs us that the editors of the *Atlantic* received, in February 1866, from the Reverend Mr. Hitchcock, a letter enclosing the macaronic verses in Latin that were rapped out on the evening of the past Thursday by what claimed to be the spirit of the deceased Parson Wilbur.

Biglow IX purports to present some few fragments of the late Parson's thoughts, in answer to innumerable requests. They are the best that can be selected from the quantity that were written on the backs of envelopes and in a very cramped chirography. For example: "It is singular how impatient men are with overpraise of others, how patient with overpraise of themselves; and yet the one does them no injury while the other may be their ruin." "Attention is the stuff that memory is made of, and memory is accumulated genius."[24]

Conspicuously missing from Number X is any prose introduction. There is not even a note from the *Atlantic* editors. The entire paper is a letter in verse from Hosea Biglow. Hosea has been asked to write something light and cute, but he finds it impossible to get into a light mood. As he looks about and "roun the hearth" and sees empty places, they set him "thinkin'."

> "Rat-tat-tat-tattle thru the street
>   I hear the drummers makin' riot,
> An' I set thinkin' o' the feet
>   Thet follered once an' now are quiet."—
> "Why, hain't I held 'em on my knee?
>   Didn't I love to see 'em growin',
> Three likely lads ez wal could be,
>   Hahnsome an' brave an' not tu knowin'?
> I set an' look into the blaze
>   Whose natur', jes' like theirn, keeps climbin',
> Ez long'z it lives, in shinin' ways,
>   An' half despise myself for rhymin'."
> "Come, Peace! not like a mourner bowed
>   For honor lost an' dear ones wasted,
> But proud, to meet a people proud,
>   With eyes thet tell o' triumph tasted!"[25]

Here Hosea is indeed Lowell expressing with deep feeling his personal loss of three brave nephews in the Civil War.

The last Biglow, Number XI, bears the date April 5, 1866. Its title is "Mr. Hosea Biglow's Speech in March Meeting." In his letter to the editor, Hosea explains that this is going to be the last paper. Then he states the "argymint" of his speech in prose. The speech, in ungrammatical verse, is all marked for applause, audience comments, etc. A considerable part of it deals with the problems of Reconstruction under Johnson and with the opposition of Congress to the President. For example, the Civil Rights Act of March, 1866, conferring extensive rights on freedmen was vetoed by Johnson after having been passed by both Houses of Congress. Very shortly it was passed over the President's veto.

However much his readers, as well as his Editor, wished for more Papers, Lowell was wise to end when he did. The principal impetus to the *First Series* had been the Mexican War and that of the *Second Series* the Civil War and the time immediately following it. Certain non-political parts of both series present some of the best pages; but, without a very strong stimulus, the style of the Papers grows quickly tiresome, skillfully as Lowell used it. No one else of his time could do this type of writing as well, but it is the kind of style that cannot survive a lessening of vitality or a loss of reader interest. At its best, it was much farther reaching than the straight prose political essays. But, if these Papers were stripped of their Yankeeisms, the contents would shrink into insignificance.

Lowell was rarely guilty of overrating his own work. By using a pseudonym, the poet had an opportunity to see how the letters were received on their own merits. He commented on this point in the Introduction to the *Second Series*:

> The success of my experiment soon began not only to astonish me, but to make me feel the responsibility of knowing that I held in my hand a weapon instead of the mere fencing stick I had supposed. Very far from being a popular author under my own name, so far, indeed, as to be almost unread, I found the verses of my pseudonym copied everywhere; I saw them pinned up in workshops; I heard them quoted and their authorship debated; I once even, when rumor had at length caught up my name in one of its eddies, had the satisfaction of overhearing it demonstrated, in the pauses of a concert, that *I* was utterly incompetent to have written anything of the kind. I had read too much not to know the utter worthlessness of contemporary reputation, especially as regards satire, but I knew also that by giving a certain amount of influence it also had its worth, if that influence were used on the right side. I had learned, too, that the first requisite of good writing is to have an earnest and definite purpose, whether aesthetic or moral, and that even good writing, to please long, must have more than an average amount either of imagination or common-sense. The first of these falls to the lot of scarcely one in several generations; the last is within the reach of many in every one that passes; and of this an author may fairly hope to become in part the mouthpiece. If I put on the cap and bells and made myself one of the court-fools of King Demos, it was less to make his majesty laugh than to win a passage to his royal ear for certain serious things which I had deeply at heart. I say this because there is no imputation that could be more galling to any man's self-respect than that of being a mere jester. I endeavored, by generalizing my satire, to give it what value I could beyond the passing moment and the immediate application. How far I have succeeded I cannot tell, but I have had better luck than I ever looked for in seeing my verses survive to pass beyond their nonage.[26]

The poet's gift for humor, as well as satire, had a great deal to do with the contemporary popularity of both Biglow series and with the fact that these works are still read today. The political, satirical, and critical poet of these works was a far cry from the idealistic visionary of Lowell's early work.

When the directors of the *Standard,* for which Lowell wrote the greater number of his political columns, decided to put him on half time and half pay, Lowell was grateful, except in regard to the cut in salary; for he did not think in the same way as these men, and felt freer to assert his true opinions, such as he did in his defense of the Wilmot Proviso. During his second year with the *Standard,* he became virtually the spokesman for the free-soilers. Doing fifteen articles a year for the *Standard* gave him a facility in journalistic writing, and his essential talent for and interest in belles-lettres raised the tone of the *Standard* columns during the period of his service.

Whether people accepted all the opinions expressed in Lowell's political writings, they were attracted to them by the language and style in which they were presented. Lowell is a spendid example of Buffon's immortal aphorism that "Style is the man himself." His choice of words, his apt and concrete figures, the verve and animation rather than—except in rare instances—any violence of expression elevated his political writing often to the high level of his literary essays.

When the Civil War ended, Lowell, who had given generously of his powers to the cause, rejoiced exultantly.

CHAPTER 8

The Diplomat

NEITHER ADEQUATE APPRECIATION nor a fair evaluation of Lowell the writer is possible without an intelligent awareness of his years in the diplomatic service. These were relatively arid years as far as creative achievement is concerned, not because the genius was exhausted, but because there were the pressures of the important assignments in Spain and England. Even these duties would not have almost completely sapped the Muse's strength if Lowell's personal life had not again fallen under heavy shadows. It was in his dispatches, his addresses, and his conversations, all of which measured up to the high tone of his literary works, that he endeared himself to these two vastly different peoples and established a relationship for his nation with them that did more far-reaching things for both than any poems or essays could have done. The letters are numerous; and certain addresses, such as the epoch-making one on Democracy, are among his best work.

I *The Spanish Mission (1877-1880)*

"In charmed communion with his dual mind
He wandered Spain, . . ."[1]

Lowell's first diplomatic mission was his assignment in 1877 to the legation in Madrid. Far from being the easy assignment that some thought it to be, it was one that required on the part of the appointee a detailed and thorough knowledge of the constantly shifting government and policies of Spain in the forty or fifty preceding years, the ability to adjust to the *mañana* attitude of the people, and to appreciate a rich background in their culture, literature, and language. Here, indeed, in the words of Emerson, if one would acquire the wealth of the Indies, he must bring the wealth of the Indies with him. This Lowell did. He learned Spanish twenty years before when he was assigned to the post of Professor of Romance Languages at Harvard, but he regretted his inability to use the language fluently. By working diligently with a tutor, he was able two months later to speak and write with ease.

When he and Mrs. Lowell arrived in Madrid, the Bourbon family was again in power, the Republic of a few years' duration having just given way. Young King Alfonso XII was on the throne. His rule was to be only eleven years in length since he died before he was thirty-one. He had said of himself, ". . . I am the first republican in Europe."[2] Lowell wrote of him: "Indeed, his position is a trying one, and I feel sure that if he were allowed more freely to follow his own impulses and to break through the hedge of etiquette which the conservative wing of the restoration have planted between him and his people, his natural qualities of character and temperament would make him popular."[3]

During his stay in Spain, Lowell never ceased to further his personal knowledge of the Spanish language, literature, and history. Calderón was one of his literary idols. The often repeated account of his ministerial appointment which is given by William Dean Howells in his *Literary Friends and Acquaintance* bears this out. Howells had written to President Hayes that he believed Lowell would be interested in a diplomatic post. Hayes answered that he would like Howells to see how Lowell felt about the post of minister to Austria. "I lost no time," Howells wrote,

> in carrying his letter over to Elmwood, where I found Lowell over his coffee at dinner. He saw me at the threshold, and called to me through the open door to come in, and I handed him the letter, and sat down at the table while he ran it through. When he had read it, he gave a quick "Ah!" and threw it the length of the table to Mrs. Lowell. She read it in a smiling and loyal

reticence, as if she would not say one word of all she might wish in urging his acceptance, though I could see that she was intensely eager for it. The whole situation was of a perfect New England character in its tacit significance; after Lowell had taken his coffee we turned into his study without further allusion to the matter.[4]

Lowell went to Howells' house a day or two later with the reply that he could not accept the post in Austria and asked Howells to bear his acknowledgments to the President. As he rose to leave, he said subtly," I *should* like to see a play of Calderón." Lowell the diplomat clearly manifested himself here. Shortly after this, he was appointed to Madrid.

When Lowell arrived in Spain, he was warmly welcomed by the young king and by the press, wherein he was greeted as "Jose Bighlow." Both King Alfonso XII and Manuel Silvela, the Minister of Foreign Affairs, were acquainted with his poetry.

In spite of the warmth of his greeting, Lowell, in his own words, "had a hard row to hoe at first." The feeling of being alone in the midst of a strange people, the newness of his duties, a lack of real ease in the use of the Spanish tongue—all pressed heavily on his sensitive nature. He also suffered three attacks of the gout in five months. He liked the Spanish people; in fact, he said that he felt a kinship with their *mañana* attitude toward life. In an earnest effort to become fluent in Spanish, he spent from nine every morning until eleven with his Spanish professor. At twelve, he went to the legation, where he worked until three. After a cup of chocolate, he read the paper and wrote Spanish until 6:45. Dinner was at seven, and at eight he drove in an open carriage in the Prado until ten. He retired between twelve and one.

Official dispatches to the State Department for December 13, 1877, to February 6, 1878, give vivid descriptions of the elaborate ceremonies so much loved by the Spanish. First there was the wedding of young King Alfonso and Queen Mercedes. Then, came Lowell's first attendance at a bullfight. He wrote that it would be his last—showing clearly his distaste for what he called "a shocking and brutalizing spectacle in which all my sympathies were on the side of the bull."[5] He was not carried away by the emotion and color of these festivities. Indeed, the panoply and brilliance of diplomatic dinners and receptions only made him like America better every day.

The Lowells took a two months' leave beginning in April 1878. Their itinerary covered Tarbes, Toulouse, Carcassonne, Nismes, Avignon, and Arles in France; thence they went to Genoa, Pisa, and Naples. From the last-named port, they went by steamer to Athens where they spent two weeks. As America's minister, Lowell observed very closely any points that could have bearing on international questions or affect his function as minister in Madrid. The experience enabled him to see with greater certainty the Orientalism that he had felt already in Spain. The Lowells were not back in Spain long before that country went into deep mourning for the death of its very young Queen Mercedes. Full account of this tragedy is given in Lowell's dispatch to the government on July 3, 1878, and in his personal letters.

It seemed to Lowell that Spain was making rapid advances toward the conviction that reform in the direction of republicanism was necessary, and that it required both the good will and the good sense of the entire nation. His keen insight made him appreciate the fact that time and patience would be required for the overcoming of the strong prejudices and deeply rooted traditions of the people.

The pain of his gout and worry over the diplomatic business that gave him some sleepless nights paled in the face of what fate thrust upon him. He had planned to make a hurried visit home during the summer of 1879 and to leave Mrs. Lowell at Tours. He wrote of these plans to John W. Fields on June 15, 1879; but five days later he had to send another message that they could not start as planned since his beloved Fanny was not able to travel. This sickness was the depressing prelude to a winter of serious illness. Mrs. Lowell had contracted typhus of the most dreaded type. She was many times at death's door. A doctor was in constant attendance; one would relay another. The slow recovery was interrupted by many relapses and by periods of mental aberration.

Night after night without sleep, the heartbreak of seeing

Fanny's weakness and suffering, the strain of trying to keep his anxiety and fear from showing in his letters to his daughter Mabel took their toll. Though there was less business in the summer to require his faculties, nearly everyone was away from Madrid during those months, so that he was left quite alone except for one or two friends and for his devoted secretary. He had perforce in the autumn and early winter to give his attention to a change in the Spanish ministry.

On January 20, 1880, a cipher telegram brought good news: "President[6] has nominated you to England. He regards it as essential to the public service that you should accept and make your personal arrangements to repair to London as early as may be. . . ."[7] Both Lowell and his wife were pleased. He answered: "Feel highly honored by the President's confidence. Could accept if allowed two months delay. Impossible to move or leave my wife sooner."[8] Shortly after his acceptance, Fanny had another relapse, and it was necessary for Lowell to leave Madrid alone and go to London for his presentation to Queen Victoria. This he did, arriving on March 7, 1880. His audience with Queen Victoria took place a fortnight later, after which he took a brief leave of absence to return to Madrid and bring his wife to England.

II At the Court of St. James (1880-1885)

"I hev thought England was the best that goes; . . ."[9]

When Lowell received the appointment to Spain, he approached his assignment with a mixture of eager anticipation for the exotic newness which the position held out to him and of natural misgiving in undertaking such responsible work among an almost completely strange people. As Minister to England, he looked forward to living in what was truly for him the "mother country." He was master of its history, culture, and literature to a degree that his considerable preparation for Spain could not possibly equal. Now he was even an experienced diplomat. All this did not mean that he would have no political problems to strain his perspicacity and his tact, for the troubles between

England and Ireland were to demand shrewdness and diplomacy of the keenest sort.

Much as Lowell loved England, he was first of all a devoted American, as his justly famous address on democracy was to prove beyond contradiction. Here, too, tact and a fine appreciation of the feelings of those on both sides in disputes kept him from ever asserting *his* feelings, which were those of his country, in a way that would hurt or irritate his audience. He had, as Edward Everett Hale observed, the ability to think on his feet, as well as a gift for speaking in public.[10] He always had something to say and enjoyed the saying of it. Such an ambassador exerts immeasurable influence for the good of his country by his mere presence.

The Feinian organization caused disturbance in Ireland and actual fear in England. Lowell wrote to the American Secretary on March 14, 1882, that "Naturalized Irishmen seem entirely to misconceive the process through which they have passed in assuming American citizenship, looking upon themselves as Irishmen who have acquired a right to American protection, rather than as Americans who have renounced a claim to Irish nationality."[11] Questions of this sort were difficult and were the rightful concern of the minister.

Thousands of minute and inconsequential questions were brought to the minister's desk. Many were from Americans traveling in Europe, many from Americans at home who thought the minister should delve into the genealogies of American citizens or find out whether there was inheritance due them in England. As an example, nearly a score of small notes, telegrams, etc., were involved in the question of getting the remains of John Payne removed to America from Tunis where he had died and was buried. Lowell's letters and dispatches indicate that he was sincerely interested in being of service to his countrymen. If the letters addressed to him had a courteous and intelligent tone, his replies were in kind.

Lord Granville held the post of Foreign Secretary under the Gladstone ministry from April 1882 to 1885—years that coincided with the major part of Lowell's term as minister. He was on terms of intimate friendship with Lowell. On one occasion when

Lord Granville asked Lowell to dinner, he said that he knew it was foolish to give such short notice "to the most engaged man in London." Lowell, always ready with a *good* pun, replied with the now famous words that "the most engaged man is glad to dine with the most engaging."[12]

Mrs. Lowell's health was not restored sufficiently for her husband to attempt the dinners and evening parties that the Minister is usually expected to give. She was able to receive a few friends at a time, to attend an occasional reception at court, and to present American ladies to the queen. This situation in no way limited the invitations that Lowell received from friends and groups. He was immensely popular and made many delightful and lasting friends among the English. The period of his formal duties was from the winter of 1881-82 until June 10, 1885. Mrs. Lowell died in February of that year.

Lowell felt a particular duty to the people of both America and England. It was to the people of England that he spoke at the Workingman's College in London, at a public meeting in Birmingham, or at the ceremonies held on the occasion of the dedication of the Coleridge monument in Westminster Abbey. He wished in this way to enhance their appreciation of his countrymen.

In the autumn of 1881, Lowell took a tour through Europe to Italy. Here he had a final visit with his schoolboy friend Richard Dana, who died the next winter, and with John W. Field, who with Mrs. Field had been the friend-in-need to Lowell in Spain at the time of Mrs. Lowell's protracted illness. A roster of his English friends would include all the illustrious names in literature—Thomas Hardy, Robert Louis Stevenson, Richard Blackmore, Wilkie Collins, Dinah M. Craik, George Meredith, Tennyson, Browning, Walter Pater, Addington Symonds, Swinburne, Thomas Hughes, Morris, the Rossettis, Matthew Arnold, Austin Dobson, Cardinals Manning and Newman, Jean Ingelow. The closeness of many of these friendships is revealed through Lowell's correspondence.

The warmth with which he was received in England was a special tribute to the impression he made on the English as a person. He had written some frank criticism of them, particularly in the *Second Series* of the *Biglow Papers*, in the article "A Certain Condescension in Foreigners"; and he made frank observations in the letters. These express openly his feelings about the English people during the Civil War. In an obituary tribute to Lowell in the *New York Tribune* for August 16, 1891, the author, Mr. Smalley, states that Lowell had probably seen the inside of more country houses in England than any other American who ever lived, a statement that attests to the admiration of the English for him as a man, as well as a writer, and in the best of them an appreciation of his frankness.

Lowell's quiet yet forceful eloquence was well suited to the small audiences—public or private—that he was called upon to address. He was past master in the subjects of most of these gatherings—relations between English and American ways of life, the nature of America, the literatures of both countries. Always an excellent conversationalist, he was a particular joy at the English "dinner-table" meetings. Lowell liked speaking, just as he had enjoyed lecturing in America; but he never gave careless, offhand performances.

He thought out and even wrote out short addresses, though he might make no use of the manuscript on the actual occasion. He thought too much of his audiences to begin a speech with the announcement that he had nothing to say. That sort of insincere pronouncement is no compliment to a gathering, and Lowell respected his listeners. Furthermore, he never forgot that he was speaking not as James Russell Lowell the writer but as minister from the United States of America to the Court of St. James. His wealth was in his talents and in the fine gifts of poise, tact, and intelligence which he brought to his task. He was fully aware that he faced a difficulty in maintaining his post as diplomat on the salary the government paid its ministers at that time. Nor was he in a position to supplement his salary from his small fortune.

Another illness, that of President Garfield, during the summer of 1881 put extra strain on Lowell. Not only did his sensitive nature suffer in the knowledge of Garfield's illness, but a great deal of pressure was put upon him in the many letters and oral inquiries and condolences that came to him as minister. After the President died in September, Lowell took a leave of absence and traveled to his beloved Italy. Mrs. Lowell was not able to go with him, but he had a happy reunion with the Fieldses there. It was not known whether or not Lowell would be kept on as minister after the death of Garfield, but President Arthur made no change.

These years were sparse in poetry, but writing occasional verses kept Lowell's technique fluent. Apart from his dispatches, his prose at this time was limited to his speeches and, of course, to his letters. He answered on May 8, 1882, Aldrich's request for a paper for the *Atlantic*: "If I could, how gladly I would! But I am piece-mealed here with so many things to do that I cannot get a moment to brood over anything, as it must be brooded over if it is to have wings."[13] His excellent speech on the occasion of the unveiling of the bust of Fielding at Taunton, on September 4, 1883, is in *Democracy and Other Addresses*. This and many other addresses did more to increase his stature as an outstanding American and more toward the cementing of good feelings between England and America than any amount of poetry could have done. His popularity with young people was attested to in his election by the student body of the University of St. Andrews to serve as the rector elected each year to give a single address. When some protests were lodged against his nomination because he was an alien, he wisely withdrew in order to avoid complications. He did speak at the unveiling of the bust of Longfellow in the Poet's Corner in Westminster Abbey on March 2, 1884. Two of Longfellow's daughters, who were living in England at the time, were present. The original of Lowell's reply to Alice's note of appreciation, currently in Craigie House, reads: "If you were pleased, I am also—in a measure. I was rather dejected about my speech. I had a bad headache & therefore was not in the entire possession of myself & could not say all I wished to say. With one thing I was wholly satisfied—I mean the honor done to the man I loved."[14]

April of the same year brought Lowell the honorary degree of Doctor of Laws at the University of Edinburgh, and a few weeks later a second one from his own university. He made some cogent statements on the obligation of journalists at the annual dinner of the Provincial Newspaper Society in London in May; and the same month (May 10, 1884) he gave an address on Wordsworth, in his capacity as president of the Wordsworth Society.

The most far-reaching and influential of his speeches was the one on Democracy, which he gave at the Birmingham and Midland Institute as its incoming president on October 6, 1884. Lowell was America's representative, addressing an audience of British people. It required tact and judgment to serve as he had in England as "an intermediary between the two freest nations on earth"[15] and to couch his convictions regarding democracy in terms acceptable to both countries. His concluding words are memorable: "Our healing is not in the storm or in the whirlwind, it is not in the monarchies, or aristocracies, but will be revealed by the still small voice that speaks to the conscience and the heart, prompting us to a wider and wiser humanity."[16] More aphoristic, perhaps, is this: "Democracy in its best sense is merely the letting in of light and air."[17]

How discerningly did George William Curtis refer to the address as not only an event, but an event without precedent. Lowell was the spokesman of a republic that derived from the monarchy he was addressing. It took the finest and firmest as well as the most gracious and tactful presentation of our principles to impress his Birmingham audience. As Ferris Greenslet phrased it, he gave the accent of finality to the eternal ideals of democracy. This he achieved by bringing out the essential combination of authority with popular opinion which alone could guarantee progress to democracy.

Much as Lowell enjoyed his years in England, he knew that the election of President Cleveland in 1884 meant his return to America. The loyalty of his English friends was manifested in their pleas that he remain with them. They wished him to agree to be nominated for a recently established professorship in English language and literature at Oxford. The temptation was strong, but Lowell felt deeply too the family ties in Massachusetts. There were no such ties in America to draw Fanny Lowell home; her mother and sister had died. Ultimately, the decision was made for them in a sad way. Mrs. Lowell, who had been feeling so much better than at any time since her dreadful illness in Spain, died on February 19, 1885, after a brief illness. It was not expected that Lowell's successor would arrive before July.

On May 7, he spoke again in Westminster Abbey at the unveiling of the bust of Coleridge.[18] He left England, lonely and shattered, early in June; but he was not to return immediately to Elmwood. Doing so would have been too difficult for him. Fortunately, the house was let. He went instead to his daughter Mabel's home at Deerfoot Farm, Southborough, Massachusetts.

CHAPTER 9

The Last Years (1885–1891)

"Oft round my hall of portraiture I gaze . . ."[1]

AT THE TIME of his arrival in America in June 1885, Lowell had six years of life ahead of him. In his letters of the past fifteen years, ho had referred to himself as feeling his age; yet, paradoxically, in his last years, he often mentioned an incurable boyishness in his nature. It was this latter quality that gave an ebullience to his writings all through his career and that enabled him to keep up his spirits through the many tragic incidents that darkened his path. The sickness and loss of so many of those dearest to him would have left other men heavy-hearted and melancholy.

The seven years of Lowell's absence had effected numerous changes in the small world of Elmwood, Cambridge, and Harvard. In the broader compasses of New England, America, and the world as a whole, this was equally true. Though he had learned of the deaths of cherished friends while abroad, the full realization of the void they had left was to sadden him more poignantly on his return. Feeling quite severed from his former activities, he contemplated a return to Europe. Without the absorbing interest of his ministerial work, even its troublesome problems, he was more keenly aware of his wife's absence.

He did not return to Elmwood for three years, during which period of time he lived with his daughter in Southborough; there he enjoyed the beauty of the lovely New England country and the companionship of Mabel and her growing family. In the winter of 1889, which he spent in Boston with his sister,

Mrs. Putnam, he renewed old friendships. Holmes, Dr. Howe, Charles Norton, and others were at the Saturday Club, but he saw many vacant chairs. Longfellow, Appleton, Emerson, Agassiz, Dana, Page—all these were missing; and William Wetmore Story was still abroad. The circle was definitely closing in. Holmes had written to Lowell in London on May 20, 1885, to tell him of the welcome he would receive on his return and also of the many missing faces:

> I have followed you to the Abbey, to Windsor Castle, to Eton with Mr. Gladstone, and am thinking how soon you are to be back among innumerable admirers and a multitude of friends—missing, alas! how many faces of those who would have made your welcome sweet. You have two paths open before you now in your splendid maturity, a career of ambition with its excitements and possible rewards, and an age of well-won and honored retirement from toilsome duties, with leisure for the studies and labors which you love best. Old friends will return to you, if you want them,—new friends will cluster thickly about you; all that can be done to make the old Cambridge life worth living for you will be at your call. . . . But your welcome will be without parallel, and you can choose your own companionship. . . . Of course we all hope you will come and make Elmwood classical again. . . .[2]

Ill health troubled Lowell frequently after his homecoming. He had been amazingly well in England; indeed, that was one reason for his reluctance to leave for home. Hereditary gout tortured him for as long as six weeks at a time. He spoke little of his sufferings while he was enduring them, but he liked to share with friends the joy of the usual sudden recovery from pain.

At last he returned to Elmwood, Mrs. Burnett going with him. He loved the place dearly and found joy again in the fine library, in the shady lawns and the great trees, and in the birds, about which he had written so enchantingly in early essays. But here, as at the Saturday Club, many dear faces were missing. Both parents were gone, and this beloved home held cherished memories of the three dear children who had died, of his first wife, and of Fanny.

I   *Addresses and Occasional Poems*

Lowell, in constant demand as a speaker, occasionally delivered lectures and addresses. He also published poems. One of his important addresses was given on the 250th Anniversary of Harvard College. A daring observation that he made in this speech was that "Harvard has as yet developed no great educator; for we imported Agassiz"[3]—daring because seated in the audience were more than a hundred men who had taught with him at Harvard. He spoke also at the celebration on April 30, 1889, of the triple centennial—the establishment of the United States as a nation, the Constitution, and the inauguration of Washington. His address was only one of innumerable, uninspired papers that carried the evening into the next morning. It was not until two o'clock that the newly elected President Benjamin Harrison rose to give a truly inspired address. Only the eagerness to hear him had kept the assembled audience together. Some of Lowell's addresses and poems appeared in print during these last years, many in the *Atlantic*. At the Lowell Institute, he delivered a course of lectures on the Old English Dramatists; the series was published posthumously.

His eloquence as speaker and excellence as conversationalist had made the English people reluctant to see Lowell leave their country; his conversations during the last six years made an enduring impression on his American friends. Lowell was not the type of brilliant speaker who insisted upon being center-stage, carrying on a monologue on a topic of his own selection. He would fit his ideas to the interests of those with whom he was speaking. Edward Everett Hale writes:

> I find, as I said, I am always reading with pleasure his estimate of his own work in the close of his life. It seems to me to be free from mock modesty on the one hand, as it is from vanity on the other. He seems to me to be as indifferent about style as I think a man ought to be. If a man knows he is well dressed, he had better not recall his last conversation with his tailor; he had better go and come and do his duty. Other people may say about the dress what they choose. In Lowell's self-

criticism, if one may call it so, you see the same freedom from conceit of any kind, which you see in those early expressions which have been cited as illustrations of his boyhood and his youth. If he had said what he wanted to, he knew he had. If he had failed, he knew that. But it seemed to him almost of course that if a man knew what he wanted to say he should be able to say it.[4]

His genuineness was also manifested in his scorn of the New England Anglomaniacs who advertised their British travels by attempting to put on what Professor Greenough once referred to as "a coat of Brittania plate."

In the autumn of 1885, he accepted the presidency of the American Archaeological Institute and the chairmanship of its committee to raise funds for the society's school in Athens. He was always ready to prove to Europe America's interest in the things of the mind.

One of Lowell's most public-spirited activities was in January 1886, when he lent the weight of his valuable opinion to the side advocating an international copyright bill, finally passed in March 1891. To the contention of Gardiner G. Hubbard, the most active promoter of the still quite new Bell telephone, that once an author launches his manuscript, it ceases to be his property, Lowell replied that all patents were ideas fashioned in a particular way; similarly, when an author fashions his ideas, they definitely belong to him. Another stipulation of Hubbard's was that the international copyright would tend to make books dearer. Lowell held the opinion that it would make them cheaper.

Always an advocate of breadth of learning and culture, Lowell stressed in the 250th anniversary address at Harvard that learning was of greater significance than knowledge. He urged emphasis on the humanities. Almost clairvoyantly he disputed the elective system. Many decades later, Harvard officials were to realize the weaknesses of this system and plan the curriculum more wisely. Here, too, Lowell voiced one of his most emphatic feelings on democracy at the college, which he regarded as certainly one of its strongest defenses. The first duty of the college is, in his words, to "set free, to supple, and to train the faculties in such wise as shall make them most effective for whatever task

life may afterwards set them, for the duties of life rather than
for its business, and to open windows on every side of the mind
where thickness of wall does not prevent it."[5]

Sheer inspiration produced little in the way of poetry or prose
in these last years. His reputation was established now, and his
work was in demand. Aldrich, as editor of the *Atlantic* wanted
poems from Lowell; and the poet was asked to write the introduction to *The World's Progress*, a subscription book, that in
its two volumes undertook to present the scientific and philosophical advances of the changing age of the later nineteenth
century. Attracted to this task by the remuneration it would
bring him, he wrote a quite independent essay for the Introduction, though he veered to the theme of the book toward the close
of his paper, indicating that the thought of men and therefore
their actions must be profoundly modified by the new theories
should they be accepted as Laws of Nature. The main doctrines
discussed were heredity, survival of the fittest, and natural
selection. Lowell instinctively resented these theories of Darwin
and Huxley as encroachments of science upon the humanities.

Nothing in the great address in Birmingham on democracy is
more indicative of his far-sighted and significant feelings on the
subject than what he said at the end of this Introduction. Not
only does it bear frequent quotation, but it could well be printed
in pamphlet form and distributed to people seeking a definition
of democracy, its aims, and even its perils:

> In casting the figure of the World's future, many new elements,
> many disturbing forces, must be taken into account. First of all
> is Democracy, which, within the memory of men yet living, has
> assumed almost the privilege of a Law of Nature, and seems
> to be making constant advances towards universal dominion. Its
> ideal is to substitute the interest of the many for that of the few
> as the test of what is wise in polity and administration, and the
> opinion of the many for that of the few as the rule of conduct in
> public affairs. That the interest of the many is the object of what-
> ever social organization man has hitherto been able to effect
> seems unquestionable; whether their opinions are so safe a guide
> as the opinions of the few, and whether it will ever be possible
> or wise if possible, to substitute the one for the other in the
> hegemony of the World, is a question still open for debate.

Whether there was ever such a thing as a Social Contract or not, as has been somewhat otiosely discussed, this, at least, is certain,—that the basis of all Society is the putting of the force of all at the disposal of all, by means of some arrangement assented to by all, for the protection of all, and this under certain prescribed forms. This has always been, consciously or unconsciously, the object for which men have striven, and which they have more or less clumsily accomplished. The State—some established Order of Things, under whatever name—has always been, and must always be, the supremely important thing; because in it the interests of all are invested, by it the duties of all imposed and exacted. In point of fact, though it be often strangely overlooked, the claim to any selfish hereditary privilege because you are born a man is as absurd as the same claim because you are born a noble. In a last analysis, there is but one natural right; and that is the right of superior force. This primary right having been found unworkable in practice, has been deposited, for the convenience of all, with the State, from which, as the maker, guardian, and executor of law, and as a common fund for the use of all, the rights of each are derived, and man thus made as free as he can be without harm to his neighbor. It was this surrender of private jurisdiction which made civilization possible, and keeps it so. The abrogation of the right of private war has done more to secure the rights of man, properly understood,—and, consequently, for his well-being,—than all the theories spun from the brain of the most subtle speculator, who, finding himself cramped by the actual conditions of life, fancies it as easy to make a better world than God intended, as it has been proved difficult to keep in running order the world that man has made out of his fragmentary conception of the divine thought. The great peril of democracy is that the assertion of private right would be pushed to the obscuring of the superior obligation of public duty.[6]

Not only are Lowell's statements clear; they are not limited in their pertinency to the 1880's. The entire passage is perhaps pertinent today—as is also the case with his views on state socialism, which he felt gave weak "paper promises" of security from misfortune at the expense of a man's freedom of development in character. The difficulty of defining democracy had been expressed by Walt Whitman in his *Democratic Vistas,* thirteen years before Lowell's address at Birmingham.

> We have frequently printed the word Democracy. Yet, I cannot too often repeat that it is a word the real gist of which still sleeps, quite unawaken'd, notwithstanding the resonance and the many angry tempests out of which its syllables have come, from pen or tongue. It is a great word, whose history, I suppose, remains unwritten, because that history has yet to be enacted. It is, in some sort, younger brother of another great and often-used word, Nature, whose history also waits unwritten.[7]

"Principles of literary criticism as illustrated by Shakespeare's *R.III*"—a paper read in 1883 before the Edinburgh Philosophical Institution, and included after his death in *Latest Literary Essays and Addresses*—was presented at the Union Club in Chicago on February 22, 1887, as a substitute for an announced theme of "American Politics." Six lectures on Old Dramatists, given in March 1887, at the Lowell Institute, were really readings from the plays with illustrative comments. Earlier essays in *Conversations* (on Ford, Chapman, Chaucer, Marlowe) were digressive; and Lowell proved, therefore, a maturer critic of form and art in the later essays. The earlier ones center on youthful admiration for the sheer beauty of the poetry produced by the writers he discussed.

He wrote a poem at the request of Howells for *Harper's,* for which he was well paid. It was entitled "His Ship":

> "O watcher on the Minster Hill,
>   Look out o'er the sloping sea;
> Of the tall ships coming, coming still,
>   Is never one for me?
>
> "I have waited and watched (the weary years!)
>   When I to the shore could win,
> Till now I cannot see for tears
>   If my ship be coming in.
>
> "Eyes shut, I see her night and day,
>   No inch of canvas furled,
> As a swan full-breasted push her way
>   Up out of the underworld.

" 'Tis but her wraith! And all the time
    These cheated eyes grow dim.
Will her tardy topmasts never climb
    Above the ocean's rim?

"The minster tower is goldener grown
    With lichens the sea winds feed,
Since first I came; each black head-stone
    Grows hard and harder to read.

Think! There's a dearer heart that waits,
    And eyes that suffer wrong,
As the fruitless seasons join their mates
    While my ship delays so long!"

"From among so many pennons bright
    On which the sunshine pours,
From among so many wings of white,
    Say, how shall I single yours?"

"By her mast that's all of beaten gold,
    By her gear of the silk so fine,
By the smell of spices in her hold,
    Full well may you know mine."

"O some go west and some go east:
    Their shadows lighten all the sea;
'Tis a blessing of God to see the least,
    So stately as they be.

"Their high-heaped sails with the wind are round;
    The sleek waves past them swirl;
As they stoop and straighten without a sound,
    They crush the sea to pearl.

"Wind-curved the rainbow signals stream,
    Green, yellow, blue, and red,
But never a ship with the glory and gleam
    Of the tokens you have said."

"My ship of dreams I may never see
    Slide swan-like to her berth,
With her lading of sandal and spicery
    Such as never grew on earth.

"But from peril of storm and reef and shoal,
  From ocean's tumult and din,
My ship, her freight a living soul,
  Shall surely erelong come in

"With toll of bells to a storm-proof shore,
  To a haven landlocked and still,
Where she shall lie with so many more
  In the lee of the Minster Hill.

"In God's good time she shall 'scape at last
  From the waves' and the weather's wrong,
And the rattle of her anchor cast,
  There's a heart shall hear life-long."

Plainly, this "written-to-order" poem is not anywhere near his best work. Its ship carries a full cargo of the poet's loneliness and longing in his last years, and in the emotion lies its value.

II *Preparation of Uniform Edition of His Works*

Even at his advanced age, Lowell exercised scrupulous care in preparing the uniform edition of his works, his major task during the winter of 1889-1890. Numerous revisions were made in the prose, few in the poems. Lowell was conscious of the inferior quality of much of his juvenilia. Actually, most "early poems" fail to rate with a poet's best, but they have their place in showing the promise of what is to come. It is unfortunate that Lowell did not date his poems. His reason was that dating would be authoritative and would give advantage to those publishers who were waiting to seize an author's work as soon as it was out of copyright, irrespective of whether the author were living or dead, or whether he or his family still wished to maintain possession. He wrote: "As for dates, as I have never kept copies of my books (in some of which dates were given), I could not hunt them down without more trouble than it is worth."[8]

It was a great satisfaction for Lowell to view his work of revision, and the ten handsome volumes of the definitive edition were a source of genuine pleasure. He did not consider his life work completed when the definitive edition was done. Rather, he hoped to put out another volume of scattered prose and another book of poems. He continued his reading with an alert interest and took joy in watching the feathered and furred creatures that lived in the fine old trees outside his windows. With little strength to work, he managed to do the introduction to a reprint of the first edition of Milton's *Areopagitica,* a paper on Francis Parkman for the *Century Magazine,* and a bit of trivia for the Contributors' Club in the *Atlantic.* He wrote of prose in his Introduction to the *Areopagitica:*

> . . . prose is governed by laws of modulation as exact, if not so exacting, as those of verse, and that it may conjure with words as prevailingly. The music is secreted in it, yet often more potent in suggestion than that of any verse which is not of utmost mastery. We hearken after it as to a choir in the side chapel of some cathedral heard faintly and fitfully across the long desert of the nave, now pursuing and overtaking the cadences, only to have them grow doubtful again and elude the ear before it has ceased to throb with them.[9]

In 1890, Lowell suffered what he called "the first severe illness of my life." It kept him six weeks in bed, and he was an invalid for a long period after he was able to be up and about. All journeys were forbidden. Unable to go to England in the summer, he had the joy of having his dear friend Leslie Stephen come to Elmwood. Keen, almost unbearable suffering marked Lowell's last months. Internal bleeding that had started eighteen months before death was the beginning of cancer of the kidney, which later spread to the liver, and finally to the lungs. Cheerful and courageous to the end that came in mid-summer—on August 12, 1891—he showed the fineness of character and gallantry of spirit for which he was loved and admired. His eyes had opened upon the world in stately and beautiful Elmwood; they were to close there too. He would not have had it otherwise.

Later Poems

"A Winter-Evening Hymn"[1]

COMMEMORATIVE EXERCISES, significant birthdays of friends, deaths of dear friends, nostalgic reminiscences, philosophical reflections aroused by personal experience—these were the themes of the infrequent later poetry of Lowell. In these works, largely tributes, the forms of the ode and the sonnet are dominant. The ode was used in most of the important later poems; its elastic length and varied metrical patterns made it a good choice. The broadening of life's experiences and the lengthening of life's shadows lent a depth and maturity to these works that the earlier poetry had lacked, but the reader misses at times the exuberance and youthful verve of the earlier volumes.

I The "Harvard Commemoration Ode"

One finds in the poet's own letters how he poured all his feelings into the "Commemoration Ode." The actual writing frustrated him until a day or two before the commemorative exercises honoring the war dead, at which it was to be delivered. He wrote to Richard Watson Gilder that the ode was an improvisation. He sat up all night to write it, then took it to Francis J. Child and asked him to tell him frankly whether it would do. Child, of course, saw its merit and reassured Lowell. The poem moved the audience deeply; yet, the poet felt that it should have made a more profound impression. In the short strophe ten, he alluded somewhat bitterly to what he regarded as a disdainful and critical attitude of the British toward our soldiers in the Civil War. The sixth strophe, one of the finest, and Lowell's tribute to Lincoln, was not in the ode as originally recited, but was added immediately afterward. The passage has proved to be one of the two greatest poetic tributes to Lincoln. Its only peer is Whitman's "When Lilacs Last in the Dooryard Bloom'd," which is longer, symbolic, expressive of the breadth of the nation's mourning. Lowell, in fewer lines, delineates the man better:

> Nature, they say, doth dote,
> And cannot make a man
> Save on some worn-out plan,
> Repeating us by rote:
> For him her Old-World moulds aside she threw,
> And choosing sweet clay from the breast
> Of the unexhausted West,
> With stuff untainted shaped a hero new,
> Wise, steadfast in the strength of God, and true.

Lowell concludes this strophe:

> I praise him not; it were too late;
> And some innative weakness there must be
> In him who condescends to victory
> Such as the Present gives, and cannot wait
> Safe in himself as in a fate.
> So always firmly he:
> He knew to bide his time,
> And can his fame abide.
> Still patient in his simple faith sublime
> Till the wise years decide.
> Great captains, with their guns and drums,
> Disturb our judgment for the hour,
> But at last silence comes;
> These all are gone, and, standing like a tower,
> Our children shall behold his fame.
> The kindly-earnest, brave, foreseeing man,
> Sagacious, patient, dreading praise, not blame,
> New birth of our new soil, the first American.[2]

II *"The Cathedral"*

Not until the January 1870 issue of the *Atlantic* did Lowell publish significant verse. "The Cathedral," inspired by a day at Chartres, was no improvisation, nor was it written in a single night. He wrote it during the summer of 1869, revising it frequently before publication. In a letter to Howells, then editor of the *Atlantic*, Lowell expressed his fears regarding the length. He said that the verses, if stretched end to end, would go completely around the cathedral they celebrated. He wrote to Norton that the poem first wrote itself. He did an initial version in pencil, copied it in ink, and "worked over it as I never worked over anything before. I may fairly say there is not a word in it over which I have not thought, not an objection which I did not foresee and maturely consider. Well, in my second copy I made many changes, as I thought for the better, and then put it away in my desk to cool for three weeks or so. When I came to print it, I put back, I believe, *every one* of the original readings which I had changed. Those which had come to me were far better than those I had come at. Only one change I made (for the worse), in order to escape a rhyme that had crept in without my catching it."[3]

Following its appearance in the *Atlantic*, "The Cathedral" was printed separately. After many stanzas of reflections, Lowell takes us with him, or reminds us of our own day at Chartres, and expresses for us what we felt as deeply but lacked the genius to express so well:

> Looking up suddenly, I found mine eyes
> Confronted with the minster's vast repose.[4]

> Still climbing, luring fancy still no climb;
> As full of morals half-divined as life,
> Graceful, grotesque, with ever new surprise
> Of hazardous caprices sure to please,
> Heavy as nightmare, airy-light as fern,
> Imagination's very self in stone![5]

The gray spire, molten now in driving mist,
Now lulled with the incommunicable blue;
The carvings touched to meaning new with snow,
Or commented with fleeting grace of shade;
The statues, motley as man's memory,
Partial as that, so mixed of true and false,
History and legend meeting with a kiss
Across this bound-mark where their realms confine;
The painted windows, freaking gloom with glow,
Dusking the sunshine which they seem to cheer,
Meet symbol of the senses and the soul,
And the whole pile, grim with the Northmen's thought
Of life and death, and doom, life's equal fee,—
These were before me: and I gazed abashed,
Child of an age that lectures, not creates,
Plastering our swallow-nests on the awful Past,
And twittering round the work of larger men,
As we had builded what we but deface.[6]

Much of the poem is devoted not so much to the cathedral itself as to an expression of the confusion in the poet's philosophy:

Each age must worship its own thought of God.[7]

I, that still pray at morning and at eve,
Loving those roots that feed us from the past,
And prizing more than Plato things I learned
At that best academe, a mother's knee,
Thrice in my life perhaps have truly prayed,
Thrice, stirred below my conscious self, have felt
That perfect disenthralment which is God;[8]

But faith and wonder and the primal earth
Are born into the world with every child.[9]

I, who to Chartres came to feed my eye
And give to Fancy one clear holiday,
Scarce saw the minster for the thoughts it stirred
Buzzing o'er past and future with vain quest.[10]

The final lines are an avowal of renewed faith in God, a faith that will not be weakened by good men's debate: "Of other witness of Thyself and Thou."[11] This poem is in many ways powerful. In its ripened maturity of thinking, it is unmistakably a "later poem." It would be easy to imagine this and others of Lowell's longer poems as rambling, digressive prose essays. In "The Cathedral," the scattered bits of description are very beautiful, but the greater part of the work expresses the poet's often puzzled feelings about science and religion.

III *Memorial Odes*

Three memorial odes—read at the centenary of the battle of Concord, April 19, 1875; "Under the Old Elm," read at Cambridge on the hundredth anniversary of Washington's taking command of the American Army on July 3, 1775; and the Ode for the Fourth of July, 1876—were dedicated to E. L. Godkin, "In cordial acknowledgment of his eminent service in heightening and purifying the tone of our political thought."[12] Of the Concord Ode, Lowell wrote to Thayer that its sentiment required more lyrical movement than the others: "Harmony, without sacrifice of melody."[13] His favorite was "Under the Old Elm"; in it he wrote of Washington:

> Haughty they said he was, at first; severe;
> But owned, as all men own, the steady hand
> Upon the bridle, patient to command,
> Prized, as all prize, the justice pure from fear,
> And learned to honor first, then love him, then revere.
> Such power there is in clear-eyed self-restraint,
> And purpose clean as light from every selfish taint.[14]

He defines country as:

> . . . a shape of each man's mind
> Sacred from definition, unconfined
> By the cramped walls where daily drudgeries grind;
> An inward vision, yet an outward birth
> Of sweet familiar heaven and earth;
> A brooding Presence that stirs motions blind
> Of wings within our embryo being's shell
> That wait but her completer spell
> To make us eagle-natured, fit to dare
> Life's nobler spaces and untarnished air.[15]

The climax is in the third stanza of the fifth strophe:

> Soldier and statesman, rarest unison;
> High-poised example of great duties done
> Simply as breathing, a world's honors worn
> As life's indifferent gifts to all men born;
> Dumb for himself, unless it were to God,
> But for his barefoot soldiers eloquent,
> Tramping the snow to coral where they trod,
> Held by his awe in hollow-eyed content;
> Modest, yet firm as Natures' self; unblamed
> Save by the men his nobler temper shamed;
> Never seduced through show of present good
> By other than unsetting lights to steer
> New-trimmed in Heaven, nor than his steadfast mood
> More steadfast, far from rashness as from fear;
> Rigid, but with himself first, grasping still
> In swerveless poise the wave-beat helm of will;
> Not honored then or now because he wooed
> The popular voice, but that he still withstood;
> Broad-minded, higher-souled, there is but one
> Who was all this and ours, and all men's—WASHINGTON.[16]

In the single stanza of the eighth strophe, Lowell, as he expressed it in a letter to a friend, held out "a hand of kindly reconciliation to Virginia."[17]

The third ode shows the poet viewing his country and its ideals from the perspective of the first century since its founding. There was much to be observed of so-called progress and advancement of thought. Lowell, always using the established values of the past to measure current ones, concluded with a noble apostrophe to the Deity:

> We, who believe Life's bases rest
> Beyond the probe of chemic test,
> Still, like our fathers, feel Thee near,
> Sure that, while lasts the inimitable decree,
> The land to Human Nature dear
> Shall not be unbeloved of Thee.[18]

Usually "occasional" eloquence in verse or prose is so much of the immediate event and relies so much on the character of the audience, the personality of the speaker, and the general emotion of the time that it loses most of what interested the original hearers. Present-day readers of Lowell's odes may see a need for condensation, but all these poems hold the spirit of their occasions and have the power to make these inspiring moments from the pages of history live.

IV Heartsease and Rue

The last collection of poetry prepared for publication by Lowell was *Heartsease and Rue* (1888), and he included in it a number of poems written before *Under the Willows and Other Poems* had been published in 1868.

The poems in the 1888 collection were grouped under five headings: Friendship; Sentiment; Fancy; Humor and Satire; Epigrams. The first grouping contains the most important poems of the volume. One of the best poems of Lowell's entire career, his tribute to Louis Agassiz, is first in the book and bears the date of February 1874. The news of the death of Agassiz reached Lowell when he was in Florence and in a sentimental mood. The deaths of his sister Anna (Mrs. Charles R. Lowell), of a friend, and of his cousin Amory, as well as the emotional recollections of his time in Florence earlier when Mabel was a tiny child, provided a base of deeply sentimental feeling that required only the new grief of Agassiz's passing to spark his poetic genius into action after a long period of inactivity. Following the elegiac pattern, Lowell first pours out his personal grief but merges that with a broad, universal sympathy as he proceeds. In the course of the elegy, he gives portraits of several writers whom he had delineated more than a quarter of a century earlier in "The Fable for Critics." Perhaps they are not more truly characterized in this later work, but they are treated with deeper understanding and appreciation. Of Agassiz, who died at sixty-seven, Lowell said:

> . . . go at night or noon,
> A friend, whene'er he dies, has died too soon,
> And, once we hear the hopeless *He is dead,*
> So far as flesh hath knowledge, all is said.[19]

The stimulus that Agassiz gave to scholarship in America is beautifully expressed in the final stanza:

> The shape erect is prone: forever stilled
> The winning tongue; the forehead's high-piled heap,
> A cairn which every science helped to build,
> Unvalued will its golden secrets keep:
> He knows at last if Life or Death be best:
> Wherever he be flown, whatever vest
> The being hath put on which lately here
> So many-friended was, so full of cheer
> To make men feel the Seeker's noble zest,
> We have not lost him all; he is not gone
> To the dumb herd of them that wholly die;
> The beauty of his better self lives on
> In minds he touched with fire, in many an eye
> He trained to truth's exact severity;
> He was a teacher: why be grieved for him
> Whose living word still stimulates the air?
> In endless file shall loving scholars come
> The glow of his transmitted touch to share,
> And trace his features with an eye less dim
> Than ours whose sense familiar wont makes numb.[20]

Poems of tribute such as greetings to Holmes on his seventy-fifth birthday, to Whittier on his seventy-fifth, and the longer Epistle to George William Curtis also show his devotion to his friends. The last was written in 1874, but not sent to Curtis until 1887 when he added to it a Postscript bearing that date. These additions are the best lines in the whole work and show how poignantly Lowell was aware of "The old haunts, too full of ghosts for me."[21] He missed Longfellow, "The clear, sweet singer with the crown of snow,"[22] whom he had daily loved to meet. He felt "What sense of diminution in the air,/Once so inspiring Emerson not there!"[23] And then Lowell wrote:

> But life is sweet, though all that makes it sweet
> Lessen like sound of friends' departing feet,
> And Death is beautiful as feet of friend
> Coming with welcome at our journey's end;
> For me Fate gave, whate'er she else denied,

A nature sloping to the southern side;
I thank her for it, though when clouds arise
Such natures double-darken gloomy skies.
I muse upon the margin of the sea,
Our common pathway to the new To Be,
Watching the sails, that lessen more and more,
Of good and beautiful embarked before;
With bits of wreck I patch the boat shall bear
Me to that unexhausted Otherwhere,
Whose friendly-peopled shore I sometimes see,
By soft mirage uplifted, beckon me,
Nor sadly hear, as lower sinks the sun,
My moorings to the past snap one by one.[24]

America, as well as American literature owes Lowell a considerable debt. As he said of Emerson in his essay "Emerson the Philosopher,"[25] his country should be ". . . grateful not so much for any direct teachings of his as for that inspiring lift which only genius can give, and without which all doctrine is chaff." He elevated our vernacular to the level of important literary expression and significant political satire in the *Biglow Papers*. With pen he did his country greater service in the Civil War than he could possibly have done with sword. He raised the standard of literary criticism in "Fable" and with Poe helped to save American literature from becoming completely chauvinistic. He aided the progress of democracy not by trying to define the indefinable, but by putting the proper emphasis on the need for an astute balance between authority and popular feeling. Finally, he imbued everything he wrote or spoke with the qualities of character, principle, social grace, and urbanity that marked Lowell the man.

Notes and References

Chapter One

1. Address delivered before the Copyright League at Chickering Hall, New York, November 28, 1887.
2. Horace Elisha Scudder, *James Russell Lowell, A Biography,* (Boston, 1901), II, 361-68.
3. *Letters of James Russell Lowell,* ed. Charles Eliot Norton (New York, 1893), I, 350-51.
4. James Russell Lowell, *The Function of the Poet and Other Essays,* collected and edited by Albert Mordell (Boston, 1920), p. 28.

Chapter Two

1. "Under the Willows," *Complete Poetical Works* (Boston, 1896), p. 290.
2. Lowell wrote of his beloved Elmwood, in a letter to the Misses Lawrence, on January 2, 1890:

". . . Tis a pleasant old house just about twice as old as I am, four miles from Boston, in what was once the country and is now a populous suburb. But it still has some ten acres of open about it, and some fine old trees. When the worst comes to the worst (if I live so long) I shall still have four and a half acres left with the house, the rest belonging to my brothers and sisters or their heirs. It is a square house with four rooms on a floor, like some houses of the Georgian era I have seen in English provincial towns, only they are of brick and this is of wood. But it is solid with its heavy oaken beams, the spaces between which in the four outer walls are filled with brick, though you mustn't fancy a brick-and-timber house, for outwardly it is sheathed with wood. Inside there is much wainscot (of deal) painted white in the fashion of the time when it was built. It is very sunny, the sun rising so as to shine (at an acute angle, to be sure) through the northern windows, and going round to the other three sides in the course of the day. There is a pretty staircase with the quaint old twisted banisters—which they call balusters now, but mine are banisters. My library occupies two rooms opening into each other by arches at the sides of the ample chimneys. The trees I look out on are the earliest things I remember. There you have me in my new-old quarters. But you must not fancy a large house—rooms sixteen feet square and, on the ground floor, nine high. It was large, as things went here, when it was built, and has a certain air of amplitude about it as from some inward sense of dignity. . . ."

Elmwood remained in the Lowell family until 1925, when it was bought by Professor A. Kingsley Porter, an archeologist and medievalist at Harvard. At his death in 1933, it was willed to his wife with the stipulation that the ownership should revert to Harvard at her death. She died on September 19, 1962. The Harvard Corporation designated the home to be the residence of the dean of the Faculty of Arts and Sciences. Dean Franklin Ford and his family are now settled there after the extensive modernizing and renovating. The house will also serve as the official entertainment center for the arts and sciences division. The restoration work cost approximately $130,000. Elmwood was built in 1767 for Thomas Oliver of the class of 1753 at Harvard. It was used as a hospital for Washington's troops during the Revolution and was purchased later by Elbridge Gerry, one of the signers of the Declaration of Independence, twice governor of Massachusetts, and the fifth Vice-President of the United States.

3. William Dean Howells, *Literary Friends and Acquaintance* (New York, 1902), p. 31.

4. *Ibid.*, p. 227.

5. *Ibid.*, p. 247.

6. Scudder, I, 43.

7. This house, like Elmwood, was historic, having been built in 1710. Recently a group of citizens organized to raise $25,000 to move it across the street into Saltonstall Park.

8. *Letters*, I, 79.

9. *Ibid.*, I, 91.

10. Scudder, I, 136.

11. *Letters*, I, 156.

12. *Ibid.*, I, 252.

13. Scudder, I, 342-43.

Chapter Three

1. "The Parting of the Ways," *Complete Poetical Works*, p. 299.

2. In Lowell's notebooks and commonplace books in the Houghton Collection at Harvard, many entries are made in French and Latin.

3. I am indebted to my colleague, Professor Thomas Ollive Mabbott for this pertinent anecdote.

4. *Letters*, II, 343-44.

5. Howells, p. 25.

6. Agnes Repplier, *Eight Decades* (Boston, 1937), p. 14.

7. *Letters* II, 58-59 (augmented ed. in three vols.).

8. *Letters,* I, 344.
9. Ferris Greenslet, *James Russell Lowell* (Boston, 1905), p. 171.
10. *Ibid.,* p. 182.

Chapter Four

1. "Eurydice," *Complete Poetical Works,* p. 88.
2. *Letters,* I, 113.
3. Forenote in *Complete Poetical Works,* p. 49.
4. *Ibid.,* p. 67.
5. *Ibid.,* p. 68.
6. *Ibid.*
7. "Spenser," *Among My Books* (Boston, 1876), II, 125.
8. *Ibid.,* II, 126.
9. *Ibid.,* II, 130.
10. Greenslet, p. 297.
11. This is taken from the prefatory notes to the poems printed in the *Complete Poetical Works,* p. 27.
12. Foreword to "The Vision" in *ibid.,* p. 106.
13. *Ibid.,* p. 107.
14. *Ibid.,* p. 111.
15. Howells, p. 24.
16. John T. Morse, Jr., *Life and Letters of Oliver Wendell Holmes* (Boston, 1896), II, 110-11.
17. Forenote in *Complete Poetical Works,* p. 106.
18. Leon Howard, *A Victorian Knight Errant* (Berkeley, 1952), p. 206.
19. *Letters,* II, 8.
20. *Letters,* I, 72.

Chapter Five

1. Oliver Wendell Holmes in memorial poem to Lowell, *Complete Poetical Works* (Boston, 1895), p. 296.
2. *Ibid.,* p. 113. Forenote to the poem.
3. *Letters,* I, 128.
4. *Ibid.,* I, 131.
5. *Ibid.,* I, 221.
6. *Ibid.,* I, 416-17.
7. Scudder, I, 162.
8. *Letters,* I, 99.
9. I am indebted to Professor T. O. Mabbott for this item #959, in the American Art Association Catalogue, April 28-9, 1924.

10. *Complete Poetical Works,* p. 140.
11. Morse, II, 107-8.
12. *Complete Poetical Works,* p. 145.
13. *Letters,* I, 348.
14. *Ibid.,* I, 242.
15. *Ibid.,* I, 377.
16. *Ibid.,* II, 272.
17. "Essay on Dryden," *Among My Books,* 1st Series (Boston, 1898), p. 51.
18. "Essay on Shakespeare," *ibid.,* p. 173.
19. *Letters,* II, 145.
20. *Writings . . . in Prose,* Riverside ed. (Boston, 1892), VII, 64.
21. *Ibid.,* VII, 68.
22. *Ibid.,* VII, 69.
23. *Ibid.,* VII, 75-76.
24. Scudder, I, 373.
25. Thomas W. Higginson, *Old Cambridge* (New York, 1899), p. 196.
26. Edward Everett Hale, *James Russell Lowell and His Friends,* (Boston, 1899), p. 277.
27. Howells, p. 24.

Chapter Six

1. Barrett Wendell, *Stelligeri and Other Essays* (New York, 1893), p. 217.
2. Scudder, I, 375-76.
3. Lowell said this in a fragmentary lecture on the study of literature, published in the *Harvard Crimson* three years after his death.
4. M. A. De Wolfe Howe, *Barrett Wendell and His Letters* (Boston, 1924), p. 28.
5. This essay appeared first in *Scribner's Magazine,* November, 1891, pp. 203-17. It was printed anonymously.
6. Wendell, p. 212.
7. *Ibid.,* p. 214.
8. *Ibid.,* p. 217.
9. Scudder, I, 390.
10. *Letters,* I, 339, August 1, 1864.
11. *Letters,* II, 275.
12. Barrett Wendell, *A Literary History of America* (New York, 1931), p. 406.
13. *Letters,* I, 276, January 30, 1857.

14. *Ibid.*, I, 281-82.
15. *Ibid.*, I, 138, September 3, 1848.
16. *Ibid.*, I, 117.
17. *Ibid.*, I, 305.
18. *Letters*, II, 114.

Chapter Seven

1. Introduction to *Biglow Papers, Series One, Complete Poetical Works*, p. 176.
2. Scudder, II, 388-89.
3. Pre-notes, *Complete Poetical Works*, p. 166. Also *Letters*, I, 296-97, September 13, 1859.
4. *Ibid.*
5. *Ibid.*, p. 119
6. *Complete Poetical Works, Biglow Papers, Series One*, No. I, p. 181.
7. *Ibid., Biglow III*, p. 189.
8. *Ibid., Biglow VI*, p. 202.
9. *Ibid., Biglow VII*, pp. 204-5.
10. *Ibid., Biglow IX*, p. 214.
11. Greenslet, p. 84.
12. *Ibid.*, pp. 86-87.
13. *Letters*, I, 320.
14. *Ibid.*
15. *Ibid.*, I, 267.
16. Appendix, *Complete Poetical Works*, p. 441.
17. *Ibid.*, p. 442.
18. *Ibid., Biglow Papers, Series Two*, No. II, p. 239.
19. *Ibid., Biglow IV*, p. 249.
20. *Ibid., Biglow V*, p. 259.
21. *Ibid., Biglow VI*, p. 262.
22. *Ibid.*, p. 265.
23. *Ibid., Biglow VII*, p. 267.
24. *Ibid., Biglow IX*, pp. 274-75.
25. *Ibid., Biglow X*, p. 276.
26. Appendix, *ibid.*, pp. 441-42.

Chapter Eight

1. *Complete Poetical Works*, p. 406.
2. Hale, p. 223.
3. *Ibid.*, p. 224.

4. Howells, p. 238.
5. Scudder, II, 235.
6. This was President Garfield.
7. Hale, p. 234.
8. *Ibid.*
9. *Complete Poetical Works, Biglow Papers, Second Series,* p. 236.
10. Hale, p. 239.
11. *Ibid.,* p. 242.
12. *Ibid.,* p. 240.
13. *Letters,* II, 267.
14. There is a small collection of Lowell material at Craigie House.
15. Scudder, II, 314.
16. *Ibid.,* II, 315.
17. *Ibid.,* II, 317.
18. The *London Times* of Wednesday, November 29, 1893, carried an account of the unveiling by Leslie Stephen, on the previous day, of a memorial to Lowell placed at the entrance of the Chapterhouse of the Abbey. This tribute consists of a stained glass window and beneath it a bust of the poet. Approximately seventy years later, on Sunday, May 19, 1963, the *New York Times* reported the unveiling by the United States Ambassador to Italy, Frederick Reinhardt, of a plaque in the Palazzo Vecchio in Florence to record Lowell's five-month stay there in 1855.

Chapter Nine

1. "My Portrait Gallery," *Complete Poetical Works,* p. 403.
2. Morse, II, 133-34.
3. Hale, p. 268.
4. *Ibid.,* p. 273.
5. Scudder, II, 341.
6. *Ibid.,* pp. 347-49.
7. Walt Whitman, "Democratic Vistas" in *American Prose and Poetry,* ed. by Norman Foerster, (Boston, 1947), p. 921.
8. Scudder, II, 395.
9. *Ibid.,* II, 398-99.

Chapter Ten

1. *Complete Poetical Works,* p. 320.
2. *Ibid.,* p. 344.
3. Forenote, *ibid.,* p. 350.

4. *Ibid.*, p. 352.
5. *Ibid.*, p. 353.
6. *Ibid.*
7. *Ibid.*, p. 355.
8. *Ibid.*
9. *Ibid.*, p. 357.
10. *Ibid.*, p. 358.
11. *Ibid.*, p. 360.
12. *Ibid.*
13. Forenote to *Ode*, ibid., p. 361.
14. *Ibid.*, p. 365.
15. *Ibid.*, p. 366.
16. *Ibid.*, p. 367.
17. Forenote to "Under the Old Elms," *ibid.*, p. 364.
18. *Ibid.*, p. 373.
19. *Ibid.*, p. 380.
20. *Ibid.*, p. 381.
21. "Postscript, 1887" to "An Epistle to George William Curtis," *ibid.*, p. 391.
22. *Ibid.*
23. *Ibid.*
24. The manuscript of these lines was kindly lent me by Professor Arthur Sweeney of Hunter College. It was presented by Lowell to Professor Sweeney's grandmother, whose first husband was Lowell's dear friend, William Page, the painter.
25. First published in the *Atlantic* (February, 1861); revised for the *Nation* (November 12, 1868).

Selected Bibliography

PRIMARY SOURCES

The Writings of James Russell Lowell in Prose and Poetry. Riverside Edition. 10 volumes. Boston: Houghton, Mifflin, 1890. The definitive text of the essays and poems, which Lowell himself prepared for collected publication. Supplemented by *Latest Literary Essays and Addresses,* ed. C. E. Norton, Boston: Houghton, Mifflin, 1892.

Letters of James Russell Lowell, ed. Charles Eliot Norton. 2 vols. Boston: Houghton, Mifflin; New York: Harper & Brothers, 1893.

Last Poems. Boston: Houghton, Mifflin, 1895.

The Complete Poetical Works of James Russell Lowell. Cambridge Edition. Boston: Houghton, Mifflin, 1897. Edited by H. E. Scudder. This work contains all the poems, including the *Last Poems.*

Lectures on English Poets. Cleveland: The Rowfant Club, 1897. This private reprint contains the reports of Lowell's twelve lectures that he gave at the Lowell Institute in Boston in 1855, as they appeared in the *Boston Advertiser.*

Impressions of Spain, compiled by J. B. Gilder, with an introduction by A. A. Adee. Boston: Houghton, Mifflin, 1899. Six letters written by Lowell as Minister to Spain and addressed to the Secretary of State.

Early Prose Writings of James Russell Lowell, with a prefatory note by Dr. Edward Everett Hale and an introduction by Walter Littlefield. London: Lane, 1902. Ten minor prose pieces first printed in the *Boston Miscellany* and *Pioneer.*

The Anti-Slavery Papers of James Russell Lowell, ed. William Belmont Parker. 2 vols. Boston: Houghton, Mifflin, 1902. A collection of periodical articles on the issue of Slavery in the 1840's and early 1850's.

The Complete Writings of James Russell Lowell. Elmwood Edition. 16 vols. Boston: Riverside Press, 1904. The first thirteen volumes reprint the text and contents of the Riverside Edition. The last three contain the Norton edition of the letters.

The Function of the Poet, and Other Essays, collected and edited by Albert Mordell. Boston: Houghton, Mifflin, 1920. An important collection of eighteen prose pieces: five lectures, twelve book reviews on old and contemporary authors, and one humorous essay.

New Letters of James Russell Lowell, ed. Mark A. De Wolfe Howe. New York: Harper & Brothers, 1932.

SECONDARY SOURCES

BEATTY, RICHMOND CROOM. *James Russell Lowell.* Nashville: University of Tennessee Press, 1942. A study based on probably the most thorough examination of manuscripts, copy-books, etc. It criticizes, at times severely, Lowell's political and literary judgments.

BLAIR, WALTER. "A Brahmin Dons Homespun," *Horse Sense in American Humor.* Chicago: The University of Chicago Press, 1942. Considers Lowell in relation to the American traditions of humor.

BOYNTON, PERCY H. "Lowell and His Times," *New Republic,* XVIII (1919), 112-14. A careful weighing of Lowell's qualities as an American who upheld the finer aspects of democracy.

BROOKS, VAN WYCK. *The Flowering of New England.* New York: Dutton, 1937. Lowell the poet, pp. 311-22, and Lowell the essayist, pp. 512-25. Interesting reading, but unsympathetic toward Lowell.

CLARK, HARRY HAYDEN. "Lowell—Humanitarian Nationalist, or Humanist?," *Studies in Philology,* XXVII (1930), 415-41. A keenly critical and deeply appreciative evaluation of Lowell's basic principles of thought.

CLARK, HARRY HAYDEN, and NORMAN FOERSTER. "Lowell's Mental Growth," *James Russell Lowell: Representative Selections.* Introduction, Part I. New York: American Book Company, 1947.

CLARK, WILLIAM SMITH. *Lowell: Essays, Poems, and Letters.* 2nd ed. New York: Odyssey Press, 1947. Introduction, pp. xv-xlix. A compact, soundly critical, yet appreciative estimate of Lowell as a man and as a man of letters.

Commemoration of the Centenary of the Birth of James Russell Lowell. New York, 1919. A collection of tributes by American men of letters.

COOKE, GEORGE WILLIS. *A Bibliography of James Russell Lowell.* Boston: Houghton, Mifflin Company, 1906. Excellent as of its date. There have been a few important studies since.

Selected Bibliography

DUBERMAN, MARTIN. *James Russell Lowell*. Boston: Houghton, Mifflin, 1966. Particularly valuable in providing a historian's evaluation of the political writings and activities of Lowell.

FOERSTER, NORMAN. *Nature in American Literature*. New York: Russell and Russell, 1923. Chapter V (pp. 111-56) on Lowell.

————. *American Criticism*. Boston: Houghton, Mifflin, 1928. Chapter III on Lowell. Not favorable.

GREENSLET, FERRIS. *James Russell Lowell*. Boston: Houghton, Mifflin, 1905. A.M.L. series biography. Clear, scholarly, readable, with two especially valuable summing-up chapters at the end.

————. *The Lowells and Their Seven Worlds*. Boston: Houghton, Mifflin, 1946. A full and fascinating genealogical account of the Lowells in America.

HALE, EDWARD EVERETT, JR. *James Russell Lowell and His Friends*. Boston: Houghton, Mifflin, 1899. A particularly readable presentation not only of Lowell but of those illustrious persons he counted among his friends. The book is valuable, too, for the excellent illustrations.

HIGGINSON, THOMAS WENTWORTH. *Old Cambridge*. New York: Macmillan, 1900. Valuable as a background book and for the intimate portrait of Lowell by a contemporary.

HOWARD, LEON. *A Victorian Knight Errant, a study of the early career of James Russell Lowell*. Berkeley: University of California Press, 1952. A closely analytical study of the early work. If carried through his life, this sort of detailed work could prove a valuable source book for later scholars.

HOWE, MARK A. DE WOLFE. *Memories of a Hostess: a Chronicle of Eminent Friendships Drawn Chiefly from the Diaries of Mrs. James T. Fields*. Boston: Atlantic Monthly Press, 1922. Interesting glimpses of Lowell with his intimates in Boston.

————. *Barrett Wendell and His Letters*. Boston: Atlantic Monthly Press, 1924. Contains valuable pages on Lowell as a teacher.

HOWELLS, WILLIAM DEAN. *Literary Friends and Acquaintance*. New York: Harper & Brothers, 1902. Part VII, Studies of Lowell, his personality, his surroundings, and people connected with his later life.

JAMES, HENRY. "James Russell Lowell," *Essays in London and Elsewhere*. New York: Harper & Brothers, 1893. Personal reminiscences of Lowell in England. Praises the poet highly.

————. "Conversations with Mr. Lowell," *Atlantic Monthly*, LXXIX (1897), 127-30. Affectionate reminiscence of cherished meetings with Lowell.

————. "James Russell Lowell," *Library of the World's Best Literature,* XXIII. New York: The International Society, 1896. A comprehensive and laudatory summing up of Lowell as a man of letters.

————. "Lowell's Temperament," *Atlantic Monthly,* XC (1902), 862-64. Short, but perceptive.

MORSE, JOHN T., Jr. *Life and Letters of Oliver Wendell Holmes.* 2 vols. Boston: Houghton, Mifflin, 1896.

PARRINGTON, VERNON L. "James Russell Lowell, Cambridge," *The Romantic Revolution in America* (vol. II of *Main Currents in American Thought*). New York: Harcourt, Brace, 1927, pp. 446 ff. A searching and, on the whole, an unfavorable analysis of Lowell the intellectual.

QUINN, ARTHUR HOBSON (ed.). *Literature of the American People, An Historical and Critical Survey.* New York: Appleton-Century-Crofts, 1951. Part II: The Establishment of A National Literature. Chap. 23, Patrician Democracy, pp. 374-84; Chap. 24, The Foundation of Criticism, pp. 384-423; Chap. 25, Literature, Politics, and Slavery, pp. 423-66.

REILLY, JOSEPH J. *James Russell Lowell as a Critic.* New York: Putnam, 1915. Exhaustive and disparaging.

SCUDDER, HORACE ELISHA. *James Russell Lowell: a Biography.* 2 vols. Boston: Houghton, Mifflin, 1901. The standard life. Thorough and scholarly.

SMALLEY, GEORGE W. "Mr. Lowell in England," *Harper's Magazine,* XCII (1896), pp. 788-801. An intimate memoir.

STEPHEN, LESLIE. Letter to Charles Eliot Norton with reminiscences and appreciation of Lowell. This is printed as an appendix to volume I of Norton's edition of the Letters.

STILLMAN, WILLIAM JAMES. "A Few of Lowell's Letters," *The Old Rome and the New.* Boston: Houghton, Mifflin, 1898. Chiefly on Lowell the man.

————. *Autobiography of a Journalist.* 2 vols. Boston: Houghton, Mifflin, 1901. More critical than his earlier essay.

TRYON, WARREN STENSON. *Parnassus Corner: A Life of James T. Fields, Publisher to the Victorians.* Boston: Houghton, Mifflin, 1963. Bits on Lowell the Editor.

UNDERWOOD, FRANCIS H. *The Poet and the Man: Recollections and Appreciations of James Russell Lowell.* Boston: Lee & Shepard, 1893. Memoir of a Cambridge intimate.

WENDELL, BARRETT. *A Literary History of America.* New York:

Scribner's, 1931. A completely unbiased presentation, indicating virtues and faults.

————. "Mr. Lowell as a Teacher," *Stelligeri and Other Essays.* New York: Scribner's, 1893. Portrait of Lowell as a professor by a distinguished pupil.

WILKINSON, W. C. "Mr. Lowell's Prose," *Scribner's Monthly*, IV (1872), 75-86; 227-37; 339-45. Prejudiced but thorough exposition of Lowell's shortcomings as critic and stylist. First important adverse comment on his writings.

WURFL, GEORGE. "Lowell's Debt to Goethe," *The Pennsylvania State College Studies,* Vol. I, No. 2 (1936). An important monograph on Lowell's great interest in and indebtedness to Goethe.

Index

Agassiz, Louis, 51, 125; *see also* "Ode to Agassiz"

Briggs, Charles F., 33, 34, 38, 60, 61, 62, 63, 78, 82
Bryant, William Cullen, 19, 22, 62
Burnett, Edward, 51

Carter, Robert, 32
Child, Francis J., 119
Curtis, George William, 126

Dana, Richard, 103

Emerson, Ralph Waldo, 20, 22, 28, 29, 45, 51, 64, 76

Fields, J. T., 87
Frost, Rev. Barzillai, 28
Fuller, Margaret, 33, 38, 62

Gay, Sydney, 53
Gilder, Richard Watson, 119
Godkin, E. L., 123

Hale, Edward Everett, 111
Hawthorne, Nathaniel, 20, 22, 45
Hazer, I. Henry, 64
Higginson, Col. Thomas Wentworth, 27
Holmes, Carter, 44
Holmes, John, 39, 44, 51
Holmes, Oliver Wendell, 20, 22, 42, 59, 60, 110
Howe, Dr. Estes, 43, 44, 110
Howells, William Dean, 23, 26, 44, 59, 98, 115
Hubbard, Gardiner G., 112

Longfellow, Henry Wadsworth, 20, 22, 27, 36, 38, 41, 42, 45, 56, 63, 72, 126
Loring, G. B., 57

Lowell, Anna (sister), 125
Lowell, Blanche (daughter), 34, 35
Lowell, Rev. Charles (father), 25-26, 28-29, 38, 43
Lowell, Frances Dunlap (second wife), 43, 100, 103, 106-7
Lowell, Harriet Traill Spence (mother), 25, 37
Lowell, James Russell, birth and parentage, 19, 20, 25; as lecturer and orator, 21-23, 41, 42, 105-6, 111, 112, 115; literary tastes, 25, 27, 30, 31, 55, 56, 77-78, 98; as diplomat, 26, 97-100, 101-7; as teacher, 27, 42, 43-44, 51, 71-79 *passim*, 98, 105; education, 27, 28, 29, 31-32; family life, 26, 29-30, 34, 35, 39, 41, 43, 128n2; political activities, 29, 30, 31, 35, 47-48, 51, 81-95 *passim*; as editor and journalist, 32, 35, 37-38, 44-46, 47, 48, 49, 117-18; travels, 38-39, 42-43, 50, 51, 100, 103; last illness and death, 118; general evaluation of, 127

WRITINGS OF:

POEMS: "Cathedral, The," 50, 53, 121-23; "Changeling, The," 35; "Epistle to George William Curtis, An," 126-27; "Fable for Critics, The," 20, 35, 36, 53, 58, 61-65, 77, 125, 127; "First Snowfall, The," 35; "Fitz Adam's Story," 38; "Glance Behind the Curtain, A," 33, 54; "Harvard Commemoration Ode," 36, 71, 119-20; "His Ship," 115-17; "Indian Summer Reverie, An," 36; "Irene," 54; "Legend of Brittany, A," 33, 57; *Nooning, The* (unfinished long narrative), 38; "Ode for the Fourth of July,"

Index

811.3
M 145

74193